THE
Grandiloquent
Dictionary

THE Grandiloquent Dictionary

by Russell Rocke

PRENTICE-HALL, INC., ENGLEWOOD CLIFFS, N.J.

Many of the illustrations in this
book appear through the courtesy of
Dover Publications, Inc., New York.

The Grandiloquent Dictionary by Russell Rocke
Copyright © 1972 by Russell Rocke

ISBN: 0-13-363291-1

ISBN: 0-13-363309-8 pbk.

Library of Congress Catalog Card Number: 70-170028

Printed in the United States of America *T*

Prentice-Hall International, Inc., London
Prentice-Hall of Australia, Pty. Ltd., North Sydney
Prentice-Hall of Canada, Ltd., Toronto
Prentice-Hall of India Private Ltd., New Delhi
Prentice-Hall of Japan, Inc., Tokyo

TO
SANDE ROCKE
AN
ORIGINAL MAN

ACKNOWLEDGMENT

I am indebted to Natalie Meltzer for her assistance and good counsel.

Contents

THE
Grandiloquent
Dictionary

Man is the wordmaking animal. As a baby, he learns what *no* means, and as soon as he is able to talk, begins using *no* right back. Later he makes the amazing discovery that parents can be completely disarranged by any number of simple one-syllable words, most of which he will later learn to spell with four letters. Still later comes high-school language courses—and spectacular new possibilities for him to insult his friends without their knowing it. Word-love strikes each human being at one time or another; but unfortunately, only occasionally does he continue to cultivate his first infatuation. Perhaps he has never had a chance to sample the dizzying richness, the savor, the *clout* that the English language has to offer, has never realized that if our words are drab and uninteresting, we are the same. But if they are vigorous, exciting, and as infinite and delightful in variety as life itself, then we too shall excite and delight.

It is often with words as with people. Sometimes a homely one is popular and useful, and one that is beautiful is only suitable to gaze upon, being of no real help in the affairs of life. *Nice, swell, lovely,* and *fine* are unquestionably *au courant.* They are also overworked, and no longer have any precise meaning. On the other hand, a word such as *anthropophagism* (the eating of human flesh) is as cadent and precise a mouthful as you could ever hope to choose. Yet, unless you are an unregenerate savage fresh from Borneo or Newark, you might not have much occasion to use it.

The well-known *disestablishmentarianism* and *philotheoparoptesism* are two other prime examples of beautiful specimens of limited usefulness. The former pertains to the discontinuance of any long-established institutional relation, and the beliefs and theories that are set up in support of such discontinuance. The latter refers to the process of cooking without haste those who have suffered the church's displeasure! But how well "sesquipedal" words restore some of the poetry and swing to language. Our enjoyment of them is not diminished by their impracticality any more than one's appreciation of beautiful people is diminished by their inaccessibility. Words as well can be admired simply for their potential . . . not to mention charm, oddity, and exotic beauty. Words have colors and textures flowers shall never know. And whether soft and gentle or wonderfully strong, they are gratifying to assemble and ponder.

I do not mean to suggest, though, that only erudite words of unusual length are counted among the most elegant and fine-sounding in the language. If fidelity to the concepts they represent is the measure, words such as *splash, squeak, buzz,* and *hum* approach perfection. What could be more aqueous than *gush* or more viscous than *ooze*? Rhythm, connotation, and sound are always more important considerations than length.

The last of these, felicitousness (or aptness) of sound, is too often overlooked. Our age bends its knee to the printed word, but for thousands of years language was an entirely verbal phenomenon. Words were preserved and perpetuated only insofar as they appealed to man's inner feeling for syllable and rhythm. This oral tradition is no longer predominant—and most of our "ears for the language" have become deaf—or at least substantially tinned. Many beautiful-sounding words, like those above and the hundreds that appear in this volume, have fallen into general disuse. They grace the crinkled pages of arid lexicons, their perfume wasted on the ungrateful heirs of Greek, Latin, French, German, and Anglo-Saxon.

There are some words, indeed, whose rhythm and cadence are pleasing to the ear, irrespective of any meaning they convey to the mind. Each has its own distinct and inimitable sound . . . ranging from the ponderous rumble of *borborology* to the amiable clarity of *gnomic*. They have the power to infuse vitality, oomph, and giddyap into your sentences and make you one of the most engaging conversationalists who ever harbored a wry smile. If you will but incorporate them into your speech, their mellifluous incandescence will be yours.

This book tries to combine style with substance. If you are looking for just the right word, turn to "Shapes, Semblances, and Resemblances," "Bodily Processes and Characteristics," or perhaps "Shades of Meaning." If you want an ornamental bauble to slip in an otherwise straightforward sentence, try "Nouns of Power," "Vibrant Verbs," and "Adjectives and Adverbs of Power." The more resplendent a word, the more you should give it a sentence all to itself. But if you want to come across like Lewis Carroll in "Jabberwocky," by all means go to the recherché and the arcane in such chapters as "Esoterica" and "Sesquipeds" (just plain big words).

If you simply want to praise something, be disparaging, or stun your listeners, you probably are more interested in the connotations or "personality" of words than in their actual meanings. Thus, many of the entries have been "rated" with one or more of the eight symbols listed immediately after this Pre-Text. A pejorative, negative word such as *thersitical* is followed by a small dagger; a word that flows trippingly off the tongue, such as *titivate,* by a tiny harp; and so forth.

Language, as the publishers of expensive new dictionaries strive to remind us, is continually changing. New words have always been cropping up as they were needed, but only recently have euphemisms and deliberately fuzzy phrases, carefully stripped of all connotation—*Vietnamization, job action, pre-owned*—come into their own. Those who care to be in the avant-garde of the wordmaking process will find satisfaction in "Words of Whimsey"—examples of word-love at perhaps its purest. And for those who would like to try their hands (or more precisely, their tongues) at coining entirely new words, "Wordmaking" gives you the raw materials—prefixes, suffixes, *et al.*—from which you can roll your own.

One word of caution: The inquiring person who glosses this book in its entirety will frequently encounter strange and bizarre words, and will look to his dictionary for confirmation of their existence. Receiving none, he will ask by what species of presumption these vocables can be admitted to assume the title "word." Readers should not permit their querulous natures to stand in the way of their gratification. The principal object is to assemble the most intriguing and challenging words actually *used* (not always printed, until now) to describe them in a comprehensible manner, to categorize them in an imaginative and unusual way, and above all, to make this an entertaining and diverting journey into the backwaters of the English language, and only secondarily a scholarly dissertation.

14

Table of Symbols

☆   Laudatory (praiseworthy)

♰   Pejorative (caustic, sharp, or derogatory)

♫   Euphonious (sounds harmonious and agreeable)

↘   Cacophonous (sounds harsh and unpleasant)

↔   Sesquipedalian (long and ponderous)

♂   Of or relating to men

♀   Of or relating to women

☿   Of or relating to persons of indefinite sexual persuasion

15

Pronunciation Key

Many longer words have two or more stressed syllables. *Corporation*, for instance, has its primary stress on the third syllable, but there is also a lighter, secondary stress on the first syllable, thus:

cor"por·a'tion

In this book, primary stress is marked' and secondary".

a	as in at, fad	f	as in fuzz, bereft
ā	as in ate, date	g	as in gash, dig
ä	as in father, czar	h	as in heavy, ahead
e	as in end, rend	j	as in jive, enjoy
ē	as in easy, sleazy	k	as in key, frisk
i	as in id, lid	l	as in love, fall
ī	as in ice, dike	m	as in mother, smother
o	as in on, pot	n	as in narc, snoop
ō	as in ode, toad	ng	as in swinger, hung
ô	as in lofty, fork	p	as in pump, hope
oo	as in good, hood	r	as in rude, iris
o͞o	as in cool, tool	s	as in snatch, essence
oi	as in oil, boil	sh	as in shoot, rush
ou	as in ouch, mount	t	as in trot, hot
u	as in up, summit	th	as in threat, panther
ū	as in eunuch, abuse	t̲h̲	as in this, smooth
ur	as in urge, surge	v	as in virgin, groovy.
ə	as the a sound in aglow	w	as in wait, reward
b	as in boost, abase	y	as in yonder, beyond
ch	as in chuck, lunch	z	as in zany, crazies
d	as in dove, undo	zh	as the z sound in seizure

SICUT ENIM A PERFECTA SCIENTIA
PROCUL SUMUS, LEVIORIS CULPAE
ARBITRAMUR SALTEM PARUM, QUAM
OMINO NIHIL DICERE.

REMOTE AS WE ARE FROM   PERFECT
KNOWLEDGE, WE DEEM IT BETTER
TO SAY TOO LITTLE
RATHER THAN NOTHING AT ALL.

     —JEROME

I think I had my first genuine insight into the nature of language when I discovered that verbal descriptions of complex shapes (*oblate spheroid*) are usually unintelligible... unless one's words refer not to the shapes and processes themselves, but to what they are *like*

One

Shapes,
Semblances,
and Resemblances

(*football-shaped*). Abstract descriptions are simply too troublesome for most speakers, whereas metaphors, the use of pantomime, and scribbling are easy and usually more faithful to the speaker's intent. Consider how much simpler it is to say pear-shaped and bell-like than to describe the physiognomy of a pear or bell.

It gets tough, however, when the object is not at all like a more familiar one. In this case, the single, succinct word often says it better. This principle is all the more true for less common shapes like that of a cone resting on its apex (*turbinate*) or a container that is swelled at the body and contracted at the orifice (*urceolate*).

The chapter that follows presents some of the most fascinating, thoroughly usable, but essentially unknown metaphoric words in our language. They draw emphatic comparisons with familiar objects, processes, or qualities, thus cramming complex meaning into few words. For instance, the word *anserine* describes silly conduct resembling that of a goose, infusing the essential elements of freshness and originality. It is also colorful, vivid, and precise.

19

acerose (as′ə·rōs″) 𝖇 Needle-shaped

aciniform (ə·sin′ə·fôrm″) Clustered like grapes

aculeate (ə·kyōō′lē·it, -āt″) 𝖇 Sharp-pointed

aduncous (ə·dun′kəs) ⚔ Hooked; curved inward

ampullaceous (am″pə·lā′shəs) 𝖇 ↔ Having a more or less globular body; flask-shaped

amygdaline (ə·mig′də·lin, -līn″) 𝖇 Of or like an almond

ancipital (an·si′pi·təl) 1. Two-edged 2. Two-headed

ansate (an′sāt) Having a handle or handle-shaped part

anserine (an′sə·rīn″, -rin) ✦ 𝖇 Resembling or acting like a goose; silly; stupid

aquiline (ak′wə·līn″, -lin) 𝖇 1. Eagle-like 2. Curved like an eagle's beak; hooked

arcuate (är′kyōō·it, -āt″) 𝖇 Curved like a bow; arc-shaped

argilaceous (är″jə·lā′shəs) 𝖇 Of the nature of clay; clayey

brazen (brā′zən) ✦ Made of or like brass

bursiform (bur′sə·fôrm″) Shaped like a smallish sac; pouch-like

campanulate (kam·pan′yə·lit, -lāt″) 𝖇 Bell-shaped

caudate (kô′dāt) Having a tail or tail-like appendage

20

ceraceous (sə·rā'shəs) 🐂 Waxy

cernuous (surn'yoo·əs, sur'nōō-) 🐂 Bending downward; drooping; nodding

cornigerous (kōr·ni'jər·əs, kôr-) 🐂 Having horns or
horn-like projections; corniculate

cuneal (kyōō'nē·əl) Wedge-shaped; tapering from a
thick back to a thin edge

cupreous (kyōō'prē·əs, kōō'-) 🐂 1. Of or containing
copper; copper-like
2. Metallic reddish-brown; copper-colored

declivous (di·klī'vəs) ✖ Sloping downward

decussate (di·kus'āt) ✖ Intersecting; crossed; in the
form of the letter "x"

echinate (ek'ə·nāt", -nit) ✚ ✖ Spiny; prickly; bristling

erose (i·rōs') Irregular and uneven as if gnawed
away

excrementitious (ek"skrə·mən·tish'əs) ✚ ✖ ↔ Of
or like fecal matter

falcate (fal'kāt) Curved like a scythe or sickle; crescent-shaped

forficate (fôr'fə·kit, -kāt") ✖ Deeply forked, like a
pair of scissors

fulgurous (ful'gyər·əs) ✖ Resembling or charged
with lightning; lightning-like

21

gallinaceous (gal″ə·nā′shəs) Resembling or pertaining to domestic fowls

glutinous (glōōt′ə·nəs) ✝ ✕ Of the nature of glue; sticky; viscid

helicoid (hel′ə·koid″, he′lə-) Screw-shaped; spiral; coiled

infundibular (in″fun·dib′yə·lər) ↔ Funnel-shaped

lacustrine (lə·kus′trin) 👑 Of or pertaining to a lake

lanate (lā′nāt) Having a wooly covering or surface

lanuginous (lə·nōōj′ə·nəs, -nyooj′-) 👑 1. Covered with soft, downy hair

2. Of the nature of down; fluffy and feathery

lenticular (len·tik′yə·lər) Of or pertaining to a lens or its shape; double convex

marmoreal (mär·mōr′ē·əl, -môr′-) 👑 Resembling marble: cold, white, smooth, hard, etc.

napiform (nā′pə·fôrm″) Turnip-shaped

novercal (nō·vur′kəl) ✕ ♀ Resembling or befitting a stepmother

nutant (nōōt′ənt, nyōōt′-) Drooping; nodding; pendent

obconic (ob·kon′ik) ✕ Of the form of a cone with the apex below or forming the point of attachment; loosely, pear-shaped

22

ocellate (os′ə·lāt″, ō·sel′it) Having eyelike spots
ostreoid (ôs′trē·oid″) ✝ Oyster-like
pandurate (pan′dyə·rāt″) Shaped like a violin or
    fiddle, as a leaf
pulvinate (pul′və·nāt″) Swelling or bulging like a
    cushion; cushion-shaped
ramiform (ram′ə·fôrm″) Branch-like
ranine (rā′nīn, rə·nīn′) ✝ Frog-like

rhombic (rom′bik) Diamond-shaped
rimose (rī′mōs, rī·mōs′) Full of fissures, chinks, or
    crevices
sacculate (sak′yə·lāt″) ♏ In the form of or having
    a sac; sac-like
saurian (sôr′ē·ən) Resembling or having the charac-
    teristics of lizards, crocodiles, or dinosaurs

scabrous (skab′rəs) ✝ ✕ 1. Having a rough surface like a file

2. Lacking in delicacy; risqué; salacious

scaphoid (skaf′oid) Boat-shaped, as a leaf

sectile (sek′til) ✕ Capable of being cut smoothly with a knife

sericeous (si·rish′əs) Covered with silky down; silky

shmooish (shmoo′ish) Shape between that of a bowling pin and a pear with a small head and mustache, but capable of changing to fit any form or need. From the L'il Abner cartoons of Al Capp

sinerous (si′nə·rəs) ✝ Snake-like

spatulate (spach′ə·lit, -lāt″) Having a broadened and rounded end like a spoon

squamous (skwā′məs) Formed of, like, or covered with scales; scale-like.

struthionine (stroo′thē·ə·nīn″) ✝ 🛡 ↔ Characterized by the head being buried in sand; ostrich-like

tessellated (tes′ə·lā″tid) 🛡 Adorned with or having the appearance of a mosaic; formed of small square blocks; checkered

turbinate (tur′bə·nit, -nāt″) Resembling a cone resting on its apex; top-shaped; whorled; spiral

unciform (un·sə·fôrm′) Hook-shaped, like the capital "J"

unguiculate (ung·gwik′yə·lit, -lāt″) ✕ Bearing, shaped like, or pertaining to nails, claws, or hooves

urceolate (ur′sē·ə·lit, -lāt″) ✕ Swelling at the body and contracted at the orifice; shaped like a pitcher

24

ustulate (us′chə·lit, -lāt″) ⭢ Discolored or blackened as if scorched

utriculate (yōō·trik′yə·lit, -lāt″) ⭢ Bag-like

velutinous (və·lōōt′ə·nəs) Having a soft, velvety surface

ventricous (ven′trə·kos″) ✝ 1. Swelling out, especially on one side or unequally; protuberant
2. Big-bellied; abdominous

vespine (ves′pīn, -pin) Of, like, or pertaining to wasps; wasp-like

vimineous (vi·min′ē·əs) ⚘ 1. Of, like, or producing long, flexible shoots or twigs
2. Made or woven of twigs

virgate (vur′git, -gāt) Shaped like a rod or wand: long, slender, and straight

xiphoid (zif′oid) ⭢ Shaped like a sword; ensiform

THINGS IMPORTANT TO A CULTURE will be reflected in the vocabulary of its language. What is important to one is often laughingly trivial to another. The Australian aborigines, for example, are obsessed by the importance of kinship. Who a man is, what he does, and when he does it depend upon his position in the social hierarchy. Naturally, their language abounds in kinship terms. Similarly, the Araucanian Indians of Chile and the western pampas of Argentina eke out a pitifully sparse existence; their language has several words expressive of varying intensities of hunger. Additional examples abound: The Japanese have some forty words for what we call rice, the Eskimo have a half-dozen words for kinds of snow, while the Basque language has no word for God.

Two
Bodily
Processes
and Characteristics

Our own culture plays down kinship: We seem far more concerned with the individual's body, its use and appearance, than with his kinship or religious ties. Consequently, our vocabulary abounds in words descriptive of corporeal sensuality and physicality . . . a representative sample of which is presented herewith.

Words associated with sex and digestion go through rapid changes in respectability. We seem to need diffuse and circumspect ways of referring to them. There is nothing that cannot be said, however, provided you make ample use of Latin and Greek derivatives. This is like the practice in Greek tragedies of having all violence take place off-stage.

27

abdominous (ab·dom′ə·nəs) ✝ Having or pertaining to a distended stomach; big-bellied

ablactate (ab·lak′tāt) ❌ To wean from the breast

androgynous (an·droj′ə·nəs) ☿ Being both male and female; hermaphroditic

ataraxic (at″ə·raks′ik) ☆ ❌ Of or pertaining to freedom from anxiety or emotional disturbance; calm and imperturbable

auscultation (ô″skəl·tā′shən) The process of listening

autognosis (ô·təg·nō′sis) ❌ Knowledge of self, especially the appreciation of one's own emotional conflicts

bromidrosis (brō″mi·drō′sis) ✝ The secretion of foul-smelling sweat; body odor

buccal (buk′əl) ❌ Of or pertaining to the cheek

callipygous (kəl″ə·pī′gəs) ☆ ♍ ↔ Pertaining to or having shapely buttocks

cerebration (ser″ə·brā′shən) Mental activity; thought

comatulid (kə·mach′ə·lid) Having hair that is neatly curled

28

crapulous (krap'yoo·ləs, -yə-) ✝ ⚔ Given to gross excess in drinking or eating; debauched intemperance

deglutition (dē''gloo·tish'ən) ⚔ Act or process of swallowing

discalced (dis·kalst') Without shoes; barefoot; unshod

edentate (ē·den'tāt) ✝ Without teeth; toothless

ephebic (i·fē'bik, e-) ♂ Of a youth just entering manhood

epicene (ep'i·sēn'') ⚲ ♀ Belonging to or partaking of the characteristics of both sexes

eructation (i·ruk·tā'shən, ē-) ✝ The action of voiding wind from the stomach through the mouth; belching

girning (gur'ning) ⚔ Act or process of contorting one's face; snarling

glabrous (glā'brəs) ⚔ Free from hair or down; hairless; bald

gnathic (nath'ik) ⚔ Of or pertaining to the jaw

29

gravid (grav′id) ♀ Pregnant; gestant
gynecoid (gī′nə·koid″, jin′ə-) ⚹ ♀ Of or like a woman

hallucal (hal′yə·kəl) Of or pertaining to the big toe
hebetic (hi·bet′ik) Of or occurring in puberty
hobbledehoy (hob′əl·dē·hoi″) ♰ ♂ An adolescent
 boy who is awkward and clumsy; a stripling
horripilation (hô·rip″ə·lā′shən, ho-) ↔ Bristling of
 the hair on the skin; gooseflesh
intellection (in″tə·lek′shən) The process of understanding and apprehending; thinking and acquiring knowledge; cerebration; putation
jugal (jōō′gəl) Of or pertaining to the cheek or
 cheekbone; malar. (Conjugal—a putting
 together of cheeks??)
lallation (la·lā′shən) ⚵ Pronunciation of "R" so
 that it sounds like "L"

30

lentiginous (len·ti j'ə·nəs) ♉ Full of freckles

leptodactylous (lep″tə·dak'til·əs) ⚲ ↔ Having slender toes

macrotous (mak·rot'əs) ♃ ⚲ Having large ears

marasmic (mə·raz'mik) ⚲ Of the gradual loss of flesh and strength; of a wasting of the body

muliebrity (myo͞o″lē·eb'ri·tē) ♉ ♀ Womanhood; womanly characteristics or qualities

narial (nār'ē·əl) Of or pertaining to the nostrils

nates (nā'tez) The buttocks

neanthropic (nē″ən·throp'ik) Pertaining to the modern human species

nictitate (nik'ti·tāt″) ⚲ To wink

nuchal (no͞ok'əl, nyo͞o'-) Of the nape of the neck

nulliparous (nu·lip'ər·əs) ♀ Of a female who has never given birth to a child

omphalos (om'fə·ləs) 1. The navel
2. The central point

onanism (ō'nə·niz″əm) ♃ ♂ 1. Withdrawal in coition so that ejaculation occurs outside the vagina
2. Masturbation

phocomelia (fō″kō·mē'lē·ə) ♉ Birth defect characterized by flipper-like arms and legs, often caused by the drug thalidomide when used in early pregnancy. From the root meaning "seal"

piliferous (pī·lif'ər·əs) Having hair

platypod (plat′i·pod) One afflicted with fallen arches

popliteal (pop·lit′ē·əl, pop″li·tē′əl) Pertaining to or connected with the hollow area back of the knee

pot-valiant (pot′val″yənt) ✝ ⚔ Valiant and courageous as a result of being drunk

puerperal (pyōō·ur′pər·əl) ♀ 1. Of or pertaining to a woman in labor

2. Of or connected with childbirth

pursive (pur′siv, pər′-) ✝ Breathing with labor and difficulty; short-winded

rugose (rōō′gōs, rōō·gōs′) Having wrinkles

sarcoid (sar′koid) Pertaining to or resembling flesh

satyriasis (sat″ə·rī′ə·sis) ✝ ♂ Excessive and uncontrollable sexual desire in men

senescent (sə·nes′ənt) ⚱ Growing old; aging

spawling (spô′ling) A noisy clearing of the throat

steatopygous (stē″ə·tō·pī′gəs, -tōp′ə-) ✝ ⚱ ↔ Pertaining to or characterized by protuberant buttocks; fat-rumped

sternutation (stur″nyə·tā′shən) The act of sneezing; a sneeze

stertorous (stur′tər·əs) ✝ Characterized by heavy snoring

ulotrichous (yōō·lo′trə·kəs) ⬧ Having wooly or crisply curly hair

IT IS AN AGE-OLD HUMAN TENDENCY to substitute inoffensive, subtilizing, and kindly terms for any words deemed distasteful or indelicate. The ancient Athenians, for instance, called harlots "companions" and taxes "contributions." In more recent times, some wordsmiths have

Three

Nouns
of Power

found it necessary to cloak a certain part of the female anatomy with such oblique genteelisms as the *monosyllable, centrique part, contrapunctum,* and *postern gate to the Elysian fields* (Herrick)! The reason for all this tergiversation seems to be that concrete reality attaches itself to certain words, for a time, whereas others with identical meanings call only a dull abstraction into the conscious mind. Thus, a well-chosen euphemism transcends the unpleasantness of death, digestion, excretion, or whatever by escaping into the shadows of its cognate.

Seen in this way, our blackest words are our most admirable . . . self-sacrificing, they dwell in feculence that their brothers may pass for white.

When euphemisms are puns as well, I call them "eupunisms," such as the inscription I once saw on the door of a men's room in San Antonio, Texas: "If occupied, we have another juan."

The message here is that euphemisms (and the other) are of considerable utility and can be great fun. Perhaps, as they suggest, the things we do not think about do not fully exist. But if you do want to call that person, place, or thing by its proper name, read on.

35

accubation (a″kyə·bā′shən, -kyōō-) ♉ The posture of reclining on a couch

actinism (ak′tə·niz″əm) That property of the sun's rays which produces chemical change

aerie (âr′ē, ēr′ē) ♉ High-perched nest of a bird of prey

afflatus (ə·flā′təs) ☆ 1. Impelling and overmastering impulse; inspiration

2. Divine communication of knowledge

almoner (al′mə·nər, ä′-) ☆ A distributor of alms to those in need; one who provides charitable relief

anabasis (ə·nab′ə·sis) A military advance; an advance from the coast to the interior

anchorite (ang′kə·rīt″) ☆ One who has withdrawn from the world for a life of spiritual seclusion; a recluse

anomy (an′ə·mē″) ☩ State of lawlessness; absence of regard for law, especially natural or divine law

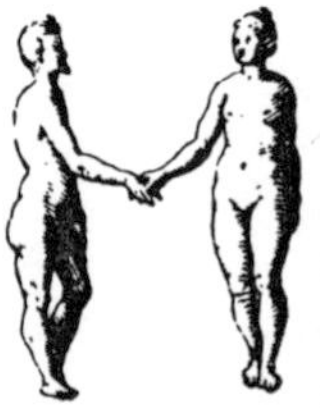

antiphrasis (an·tif′rə·sis) ⤪ Use of a word or phrase in which the intended meaning is the opposite of that expressed; that is, the speaker's words belie his intended, antipodal meaning; irony: *And Brutus is an honorable man*

antisyzygy (an″ti·siz′i·jē) ⤪ ↔ A union of opposites

aphesis (af′i·sis) The gradual loss of unstressed initial vowels, as in *squire* for *esquire*

argosy (ar′gə·sē) A large merchant ship, especially one with a rich cargo; a fleet of them

autonomasia (ô′tə·nō·mā′zhə) ↔ 1. Use of a proper name as a common noun: a quisling
2. Use of an epithet instead of a proper name: the Virgin Queen

avatar (av″ə·tar′) The carnate embodiment of a god, idea, principle, or cause, as: *The third party made its avatar in Wallace, three goose-steps to the right of Nixon*

beldam (bel′dəm) ♁ ♀ An old and haggish woman

bibelot (bib′lō) ☆ ♅ Small artistic object of beauty or rarity

bight (bīt) The loop or middle part of a rope, as distinguished from the ends

blandishment (blan′dish·mənt) ♁ Action or manner that flatters, coaxes, or cajoles, as by soft and false words

brouhaha (broo·hä′hä, broo″hä·hä′) ♁ Noisy uproar; tumultuous confusion; hubbub

37

bushido (bōō′shē·dô′) Samurai code of conduct emphasizing courage and preferring suicide to dishonor

cairn (kārn) A mound of stones serving as a monument or memorial

calligraphy (kə·lig′rə·fē) ☆ Beautiful and elegant penmanship; handwriting generally

calumet (kal′yə·met″, kal″yə·met′) Peace pipe; long-stemmed pipe smoked by North American Indians in token of peace

camarilla (kam″ə·ril′ə)  Cabal; clique; group of secret advisers

carillon (kar′ə·lon″, -lən)  Set of stationary bells, each emitting a single tone

carousal (kə·rou′zəl) ✝ Jovial drinking party; drunken revel; bacchanal

caryatid (kar″ē·at′id) ♀ A supporting column in the form of a sculptured female figure

cathexis (kə·thek′sis) ⭠ Attachment of emotional significance to an idea or object; emotional investment in things

caudle (kôd′əl) A warm drink for the sick, especially a spiced and sugared broth with wine or ale

causerie (kō″zə·rē′, kô″-) Informal discussion or chat; light conversation

charnel (chär′nəl) ✝ 1. Repository for dead bodies; burial place

2. Death-like; ghastly; sepulchral

chiromancy (kī′rə·man″sē) Palmistry; foretelling fortunes on the basis of the configuration of one's palm

concinnity (kən·sin′i·tē) ☆ Internal harmony and fitness; graceful refinement

consuetude (kon′swi·tōōd″, -tyōōd″) Social usage having legal force; custom

conurbation (kən″ur·bā′shən) A densely populated urban area surrounded by smaller cities and suburbs

coprophilia (ko″pro·fil′ē·ə, -fēl′yə) ✝ ≷ Extreme interest in feces

cosmopolite (koz·mop′ə·līt″) ☆ Citizen of the world; one not bound by local or national prejudices or attachments

cryotherapy (krī″o·ther′ə·pē) Treatment effected by the use of cold

cudgel (kuj′əl) ✝ A short, heavy stick or club used as a weapon

cunctation (kungk·tā′shən) ✝ Procrastination; delay; tardiness

curioso (kyoor″ē·ō′sō) A lover of the rare and queer as well as the usual; the true amateur

curmudgeon (kər·muj′ən) ✝ A surly, irascible, churlish, and cantankerous fellow

cynophobia (sī′nə·fō″bē·ə) Fear of dogs

cynosure (sī′nə·shoor″, sin′ə-) ☆ 1. The center of interest or attention by virtue of brilliance or keenness

2. Something that guides or directs, as the polestar

decrement (dek′rə·mənt) ✝ Process of becoming gradually less; diminution; decrease

delator (di·lā′tər) One who informs against or accuses; informer

deltiologist (del″tē·ol′ə·jist) ↔ One who collects picture postcards

disquisition (dis″kwi·zish′ən) 1. Formal inquiry into or discussion of a subject

2. An elaborate essay, treatise, or discourse

diva (dē′vä) ♀ Prima donna; leading woman singer

doggerel (dô′gər·əl, dog′ər-) ✝ Loose, irregular poetry; inartistic, weakly constructed verse

dollop (dol′əp) A lump, hunk, or blob of some substance

drogue (drōg) A sea anchor comprised of a bucket or canvas bag on a line

dromomania (drō·mə·mā′·nē·ə, -mān′yə) ⚡ An exaggerated longing for travel

dudgeon (duj′ən) ♱ Resentment; sulky displeasure; aggrieved humor

dystopia (dis·tō′pē·ə) ♱ An imagined place or period in which things are as wretched as they are wonderful in a utopia

ecdysiast (ek·diz′ē·ast″) ♀ ♂ One who rhythmically disrobes; stripteaser

energumen (en″ər·gyo͞o′mən) ♱ 1. One possessed of an evil spirit; demoniac
2. Fanatical enthusiast; zealot

epithalamium (ep″ə·thə·lā′mē·əm) 🎶 ↔ Nuptial song or poem in honor of the bride and bridegroom

epizeuxis (ep″i·zo͞ok′·səs) ⚡ Emphatic repetition of a word for emphasis

eponym (ep′ə·nim) A real or mythical person from whom a place, institution, etc., derives or is supposed to derive its name. William Penn is the *eponym* of Pennsylvania

factotum (fak·tō′təm) 1. A man of all work; handyman

2. A person having many and various duties to perform

fanfaronade (fan″fə·rə·nād′) ✝ Boasting speech; bluster; bravado; swagger

farrago (fə·rä′gō, -rā′-) ✝ Confused mixture; hodgepodge

funambulist (fyo͞o·nam′byə·list) Tightrope walker

gallimaufry (gal″ə·mô′frē) ✝ ✘ Hodgepodge; jumble; farrago

gasconade (gas″kə·nād′) ✝ Extravagant boasting; bluster; braggadocio

glitch (glich) ✝ ✘ 1. A false or spurious electronic signal

2. A malfunction or mishap

hagiophobia (hag″ē·ō·fō′bē·ə) ⬦ An excessive dread of holy persons or things

hardihood (här′dē·hood″) ☆ Sturdy courage; boldness; daring; audacity

hebetude (heb′i·tōōd″, -tyōōd″) ♰ Slow in perceiving; dullness

hogmanay (hog″mə·nā′) 1. New Year's Eve
2. A gift made to a child on New Year's Eve

ignicolist (ig·ni·kō′list) ⬦ A fire-worshipper

imbrication (im″brə·kā′shən) An overlapping, as of scales or tiles, for instance

inanition (in″ə·nish′ən) 1. The process of emptying, or the condition of being empty
2. Exhaustion from want of nourishment

intumescence (in″tōō·mes′əns, -tyoo-) The process of swelling up

jactation (jak·tā′shən) ♰ Boasting; bragging

labefaction (lab″ə·fak′shən) 1. A shaking or weakening
2. Overthrow; downfall

lagniappe (lan·yap′, lan′yap) 🜏 1. A small present given for good measure to a purchaser
2. Something given or obtained gratuitously

litotes (lī′tə·tēz″, -tō-, lit′ə-) 🜏 The expression of an affirmative by the negative of its contrary; understatement, as: *not bad at all*

logodaedaly (lô″gə·dē′də·lē) ↔ Cunning manipulation with words; verbal legerdemain

lucubration (lōō″kyoo·brā′shən) Laborious work, study, or writing, especially that done at night

mactation (mak·tā′shən) ♰ The action or process of killing a sacrificial victim

mansuetude (man′swi·tōōd″, -tyōōd″) Gentleness; meekness; mildness

marplot (mär′plot″) ✞   One who spoils a plan or design through meddling interference

mendicity (men·dis′i·tē) ✞   The practice of begging, or the condition of being a beggar

moil (moil) ✞   1. Hard work; drudgery
2. Confusion; turmoil

mugwump (mug′wump″) ✞   One who is independent or affects superiority, especially in politics

nescience (nesh′ē·əns) ✞   Absence of knowledge; ignorance

nimiety (ni·mī′i·tē)   Overabundance; excess

nodus (nō′dəs)   A difficult or intricate point; a knotty problem

nostomania (nos″tə·mā′ne·ə, -mān′yə)   Irresistible compulsion to return home; intense homesickness

nympholepsy (nim′fə·lep″sē) ↔   A state of ecstasy or frenzy caused by desire for the unobtainable

obbligato (ob″lə·gä′tō, ôb″blē·gä′tō) 𝄞   An indispensable musical accompaniment

obsequy (ob′sə·kwē)   A funeral rite or ceremony

ochlocracy (ok·lok′rə·sē) ✞   Mob rule

offal (ô′fəl, of′əl) ✞   Garbage; waste; refuse; dross

omniana (om·nē·an′ə) 𝄞   Notes or scraps of information about anything

origami (ôr″ə·gä′mē)   The Japanese art of folding sheets of paper to make various objects and designs

44

oubliette (o͞o·ble̅·et′) ♆ A secret dungeon into which prisoners are lowered through a trap door at the top

paedophage (pā′do̅·fāj, pē-) ✢ A child-eater

palindrome (pal′in·dro̅m″) A word, verse, etc., that reads the same backward as forward: *Madam, I'm Adam*

pannier (pan′yər, -e̅·ər) ♆ A large basket for carrying provisions, usually slung, in pairs, across the back of a beast of burden

paraclete (par′ə·kle̅t″) ♆ One called in to aid or intercede; an advocate

penetralia (pen″i·trā′le̅·ə) The innermost parts or recesses

philluminist (fi·lo̅o̅m′ə·nist) ↔ One who collects matchbox tops

philter (fil′tər) 1. A love potion
2. A magic potion for any purpose

phobophobia (fo̅′bo̅·fo̅′be̅·ə) The fear of being afraid

45

polyhistor (pol″ē·his′tər) ☆　A man of great and varied learning; great scholar; polymath

popinjay (pop′in·jā″) ✝ ♂ ♀ ♀̣　A vain person given to empty chatter and foppish displays; coxcomb

posset (pos′it)　A drink composed of hot milk curdled with ale, wine, or the like, often sweetened and spiced

primoprime (prīm′ō·prīm) ☆　The very first, best, or most original

putsch (pooch) ✝　A sudden minor uprising or revolt

querist (kwēr′ist)　One who inquires; a questioner

quiddity (kwid′i·tē) 🛡　1. That which makes a thing what it is; essential nature; essence
2. A trifling and captious nicety; trivial distinction

rhapsodist (rap′sə·dist)　A person who speaks or writes with extravagant enthusiasm

roisterer (roi′stər·ər)　A swaggering or noisy reveler; boisterous merrymaker

sciolism (sī′ə·liz″əm) ✝　Pretentious superficiality of knowledge

46

shard (shärd) Fragment of a brittle substance, especially broken earthenware

sjambok (sham·bok′, -buk′) ✝ ⚊ 1. Whip of rhinoceros or hippopotamus hide

2. A tyranny of oppression, violence, and whips

skein (skān) ⚊ 1. A quantity of yarn wound in a coil

2. Circumstances or undertakings easily twisted or mixed up

slough (slou) ✝ A bog, swamp, or mire

sodality (sō·dal′i·tē, sə-) 1. Fellowship; companionship

2. An association or brotherhood

stele (stē′lē, stēl) An inscribed stone, slab, or pillar used as a monument; gravestone

succubus (suk′yə·bəs) ✝ ♀ 1. A demon in female form, said to have carnal intercourse with men in their sleep

2. A prostitute or whore

succussion (sə·kush′ən) ✖ The action of shaking, or the condition of being shaken forcibly

sutteeism (su·tē′ism, sut′e·ism) The practice of immolating oneself on the funeral pyre of one's husband, formerly performed by Hindu widows

swale (swāl) A hollow or depression, usually moist or marshy, in a tract of land

tachygraphy ta·kig′rə·fē, tə-) ✖ ↔ The art or practice of quick writing; speedwriting; shorthand

tarboosh (tär·bōōsh′) A red cap of cloth or felt with a tassel attached at the top, worn by Mohammedan men; the fez is the Turkish form

temblor (tem′blər, -blôr) A tremor; earthquake

thanatopsis (than″ə·top′sis) ↔ A musing or contemplation of death

trice (trīs) ⚲ Very short time; an instant; a moment

troglodyte (trog′lə·dīt″) ♰ 1. Cave-dweller; caveman

2. Person living in seclusion; hermit; recluse

ubiety (yōō·bī′i·tē) The condition or quality of being located in a definite place at any given time

ukase (yōō′kās, yōō·kāz′) ⟍ An official decree, order, or proclamation issued by an absolute or arbitrary authority

velleity (və·lē′i·tē) ⚎ A mere wish or desire unaccompanied by the slightest action to obtain it

vivisepulture (viv″ə·sep′əl·chər) ♰ ↔ The practice of burying people alive

warren (wôr′ən, wor′-) ♰ A tenement house or populated district so crowded that it resembles the breeding place of rabbits

wraith (rāth) ⚎ Apparition; phantom; ghost

xerophagy (zi·rof′ə·jē) ⟍ The eating of dry food, especially as a form of fast

zonule (zōn′yōōl) ⟍ A small belt, band, or zone

SOME PEOPLE SPEAK ENGLISH AS though they were translating their thoughts from one dead language to another. They seem to have no feeling for the heft and variety of verbs, nor appreciation of their readiness and abundance. Instead of walking, boating, riding, driving, jogging, strolling, or ambling, they "go." They "get" a new car, a head cold, a prescription, drunk, fired, at it, and with it. *To go* and *to get* have become so adaptable that they are practically blank spaces that the listener fills in, a disguised method of verbal shorthand.

Vibrant Verbs

Verbs can change all that! Think of them as the hinges upon which your sentences swing. Ever since English dropped its inflectional system of grammar in the days of Chaucer, there has been nothing to distinguish the form of verb and noun. This means that any noun or adjective becomes a verb if employed as such, and conversely, most verbs can be used to express the idea of their action. Hence, verbs can go either way and magically infuse vitality into your speech by impressing nouns and adjectives into service. Thus, *to grease, to yellow, to table, to author, to paddle,* and *to serenade* are acceptable verbs. *Put-down, set-back, wipe-out,* and *drop-out* are equally acceptable nouns.

Naturally, the more action-packed and vigorous the verb you use, the better your speech will be. The ones that follow transform slowly accumulating clauses into quickly stabbing thoughts . . . they wriggle and shine like minnows fetched fresh from a brook.

51

abrade (ə·brād′) ✕ To rub or wear off: *Unsuccessful wars abrade the popularity of government*

anneal (ə·nēl′) 🔔 1. Set on fire; inflame; kindle: *Anneal the oven*

2. Temper; toughen: *Anneal the mind to sundry cares*

bastinado (bas″tə·nā′dō) 1. Striking the soles of the feet with a stick: *The jailers bastinadoed their prisoner*

2. A blow or beating with a stick: *They resorted to bastinado to make him speak*

batten (bat′ən) To thrive and grow fat by feeding: *The bat battened on a batch of bitter berries*

bombinate (bom′bə·nāt″) ✕ To buzz; make a buzzing noise: *Bombinating bees*

burlesque (bər·lesk′) ✝ Derisively or comically imitate; parody; mock; caricature: *Some comedians earn their livings by burlesquing politicians*

cadge (kaj) ✝ 1. To hawk or peddle, as fish: *The fishermen set about cadging their morning's catch*

2. To beg, sponge, or fleece: *Cadging nickels from passersby*

caparison (kə·par'i·sən) 1. To outfit a horse with ornaments and trappings: *Gaily caparisoned circus horses*

2. To deck finely; adorn with right dress: *Little girls gleefully caparison their dolls.*

caterwaul (kat'ər·wôl'') ✝ 1. Wail, screech, or howl shrill, discordant sounds, like a cat: *The raucous din of caterwauling felines*

2. Quarrelling like cats: *A noisy assembly of snide, caterwauling women*

confabulate (kən·fab'yə·lāt'') Converse in an informal, familiar way; chat: *The grand old professor confabulated with his students over a beer*

contemn (kən·tem') ✝ View with contempt, scorn, and disdain; despise: *Abhor the traitor and contemn his treachery*

cozen (kuz'ən) ✝ Cheat; deceive; beguile by some paltry trick: *The darkened room cozened the child into believing it was bedtime*

53

crepitate (krep'i·tāt″) ⬹ To make a crackling sound, as with sudden, sharp, repeated noises: *The crepitating clatter of hooves*

decoct (di·kokt′) Extract the essence or flavor of, as by boiling: *A proverb is much matter decocted into few words*

deliquesce (del'ə·kwəs) 🎵 Melt away; gradually dissolve: *Don't let your vocabulary deliquesce into a dozen worn expressions*

deracinate (di·ras'ə·nāt″) ⬹ 1. Pull up by the roots; uproot; pluck: *Glaciers deracinate pines*
2. Extirpate; eradicate; abolish completely: *Joseph McCarthy sought to deracinate communists from defense plants*

dilate (dī·lāt′, di-) Write or speak at length or in detail; develop diffusely; expatiate: *Many have dilated upon the evils of poverty*

discommode (dis″kə·mōd′) ✝ Disturb; annoy; put to inconvenience: *Noisy tenants discommode their neighbors*

divagate (dī'və·gāt″) 1. To wander or stray: *Don't let rambunctious sheep divagate from the flock*
2. Digress; deviate: *Politicians all too frequently divagate from the question at issue*

encincture (en·singk'chər) 🎵 Encircle; encompass; surround: *Indians encinctured the wagon train*

estivate (es′tə·vāt″) To spend the summer: *Some animals estivate in a state of dormancy*

festoon (fe·stoon′) 🎵 Decorate with a garland or chain of flowers, leaves, etc., suspended in a curve between two points: *The doorway is festooned with lilacs*

flummox (flum′əks) ✝ To confuse, perplex, or abash, always with the idea of shocking and victimizing: *Lennie flummoxed the critics*

imbrue (im·broo′) Soak, drench, or stain, especially with blood: *Scarlet bandages imbrued with blood*

incrassate (in·kras′āt) ✕ To make or become thick or thicker; to thicken; inspissate: *The cup of flour incrassated the gravy*

ingeminate (in·jem′ə·nāt″) Repeat; reiterate; to emphasize by repetition. *With dolorous chants the marchers ingeminate their prayers for peace*

jape (jāp) ✕ To jest; jibe; play tricks: *Running, jumping, and japing—the paramount joys of childhood*

jugulate (joo′gyə·lāt″) ✝ 1. To check or suppress by extreme measures: *A desperate attempt to jugulate the cancer by radical surgery*
2. To cut the throat of: *The pirates jugulated their hostage*

limn (lim) Draw or paint, as a picture; portray; describe: *The master of ceremonies limned the next speaker as a brave man*

mulct (mulkt) ✕ To punish by means of a fine: *Traffic tickets mulct unlawful drivers*

nettle (net′əl) To irritate; vex; annoy: *Petty details nettled the busy executive*

nidificate (nid′ə·fə·kāt″) ⟋ ↔ To make a nest: *Birds' ability to nidificate is inborn, not learned*

novate (nō′vāt) To replace with something new: *Their childhood pledge of fidelity was novated by marital vows*

obsecrate (ob′sə·krāt″) To entreat earnestly; beseech; supplicate: *Ministers obsecrate us to do good and shun evil*

obtund (ob·tund′) Serving to blunt, dull, or deaden: *Novocaine obtunds pain*

pall (pôl) ✝ Become flat, stale, or dull; cease to please: *Her beauty never palled*

periclitate (pə′ri·klə·tāt″) ✝ ⟋ To expose to peril; endanger; risk: *Heedless travellers periclitate their lives*

pullulate (pul′yə·lāt″) ♉ To sprout, breed, or multiply rapidly: *The population is pullulating like rabbits*

quail (kwāl) ✝ To draw back in fear; lose heart or courage; cower; blench: *David didn't quail when he saw Goliath*

refocillate (re·fos′ə·lāt″) ♉ To warm into life again; revive: *Artificial respiration occasionally refocillates an inactive heart*

retund (ri·tund′) ✝ ⟋ To weaken or diminish the strength or effect of: *Let nothing retund your efforts at word mastery*

roil (roil) ✞ ✘ Vex; disturb; irritate; rile: *Foolish questions roil teachers royally*

scout (skout) Reject or dismiss scornfully; flout; scoff at: *Law students tend to scout the hoary conservatism of their professors*

scud (skud) To move or dart briskly or nimbly, as before a gale: *A scudding rain deluged the crops*

siffilate (sif′ə·lāt″) ♌ To whisper: *Brisk breezes and siffilating pines*

simper (sim′pər) ✞ To smile in a silly, self-conscious, or affected way; smirk: *The guilty party simpered uncontrollably and gave himself away*

soodle (sōōd′əl) To walk, stroll, or saunter in a slow, leisurely manner: *Carefree lovers often soodle along the boardwalk until dusk*

sough (sou, suf) ✘ To make a soft and low murmuring, rustling, or rushing sound: *The wind soughed through the meadow in a long, monotonous swell*

stridulate (strij′ə·lāt″) ✘ ↔ To make a shrill or chirping sound, as certain insects: *Crickets seem to stridulate incessantly*

suffuse (sə·fyōōz′) ♌ Gradually spreading over the surface and serving to color or tint, as with a fluid or gleam of light: *An amused expression suffused his face*

titivate (tit′ə·vāt″) ♌ To make smart; spruce up: *Rather than shop for a new dress, Granny titivated her old lace one*

transude (tran·sōōd′) ♌ To pass or ooze through or

out, as sweat through pores: *The tree's sap transuded into the collecting pails*

triturate (trich′ə·rāt″) ⟟ To rub, grind, or otherwise crush into fine particles; pulverize; comminute: *Millstones triturate wheat*

truckle (truk′əl) ⟟ To show servility or subservience: *Do not truckle like a milksop*

ululate (yōōl′yə·lāt″, ul′-) ⟟ 1. To howl or hoot: *Ululating foxhounds*

2. To wail or lament loudly: *Ululating mourners*

unbosom (un·booz′əm, -bōō′zəm) To disclose one's personal thoughts or feelings: *One often feels greatly relieved after unbosoming himself to a stranger*

vellicate (vel′ə·kāt″) ⟟ 1. To pull at, off, or out with a sudden jerk; to pluck: *Women vellicate their false eyelashes before applying cold cream to their faces*

2. To move with spasmodic convulsions; twitch: *The dying dog vellicated uncontrollably*

vesticate (ves′tə·kāt″) To blister: *The blazing sun vesticated our lips*

winnow (win′ō) ⟟ Separate or sort out; sift; blow off like chaff from grain: *Winnow your convictions before declaring your loyalty*

ADJECTIVES AND ADVERBS MODIFY.
But nowhere is it written that they
must colorlessly immure themselves,
desolate and flaccid, between capital
and period.

Their function is to qualify, describe, and thereby give definition to
our ideas. They have the power to
evoke vivid recollections of sensory experience—smells,
sounds, tastes—and thus to call up meaning from the
wellsprings of our minds. Consider "*shiny* red apple"
and "sing *sweetly,* my love." And remember the "Tom
Swifties"—jokes that depended solely on an ambiva-
lent adverb (e.g., "Yes, we have no bananas," said Tom
fruitlessly). These words are strong medicine in their
own right, and blur everything they do not make clear.
Their touch should be light and lucid; their manner
elegant, without being artificial or finicky.

Five

*Adjectives and
Adverbs of
Power*

abstersive (ab·stur′siv) ✕   Serving to cleanse or
     purge
acescent (ə·ses′ənt)   Turning sour; tending to turn
     acid
adscititious (ad″si·tish′əs) ✝ 🝮 ↔   Not essential;
     supplemental; superfluous: *A pantheon of ad-
     scititious deities*
agravic (ə·grav′ik)   Of or relating to a condition of
     no gravitation
aleatoric (ā′lē·ə·tōr″ik, -tôr″-) ✕   Pertaining to mu-
     sic or other art forms dependent upon tech-

59

niques based upon chance. From *aleatory,* meaning dependent upon chance; uncertain; unpredictable

algetic (al·jet′ik) ⤯ Causing or relating to pain

algolagnic (al″gə·lag′nik) ✝ ⤯ Relating to the perception of pleasure from inflicting or suffering pain

allogenic (al″ə·jen′ik) Genetically dissimilar

amphibolous (am·fib′ə·ləs, am″fə·bol′əs) ✝ ⤯ Susceptible of two meanings; ambiguous; equivocal

anacreontic (ə·nak″rē·on′tik) ☆ ↔ ⤯ Jovial, festive, and amatory

anagogic (an″ə·goj′ik) ⤯ Relating to things spiritual and mystical; occult; gnostic

analeptic (an″ə·lep′tik) ⤯ Serving to renew strength and vigor; invigorating

aniconic (an″ī·kon′ik) ⤯ Not using or permitting images, effigies, or idols

anile (an′īl, ā′nīl) ☆ ♀ Old-womanish; lacking in force, strength, or effectiveness; faltering

antelucan (an″tə·lōōk′ən) Pertaining to or occurring before dawn

antibromic (an″tē·brō′mik) Causing the elimination of odors; deodorizing

apocrustic (ap″ə·krust′ik, ap′o-) ⚔ Having the power to draw together and constrict, thereby preventing discharge or entrance; astringent

apodictic (ap″ə·dik′tik) ⚔ Incontrovertibly established; incontestable; absolutely certain

apolaustic (ap″ə·lôst′ik, ap′o-) ☆ Given to enjoyment; self-indulgent

apterous (ap′tər·əs) Without wings; wingless

archly (ärch′lē) In a playfully mischievous manner; rascally; roguishly

arenicolous (ar″ə·nik′ə·ləs) ↔ Inhabiting sand

argute (är·gyōōt′) 🎵 Shrill; clear; keen

astucious (ô·stu′shəs, -stush′əs) Having keen perception; of astute and penetrating discernment: *"Why do Jews answer a question with a question?" "Why not?" asked Morty, astuciously*

asyndetic (as′in·det′ik) ⚔ Not connected by conjunctions: *I came, I saw, I conquered*

austral (ô′strəl) In or relating to the south; southern

balneal (bal′nē·əl) Of or pertaining to baths or bathing

banausic (bə·nô′sik, -zik) ☩ 1. Predominantly suggestive of utilitarian and practical usage rather than decorative or ornamental: *Architecture more banausic than inspired*

2. Common, ordinary, and undistinguished; dull and insipid

beetling (bēt′ling) Jutting over; overhanging; projecting

bezoardic bē′zōr·dik, -zôr-) ⚡ Of the nature of or pertaining to a counterpoison or antidote

bosky (bos′kē) Consisting of or covered with bushes or undergrowth

brumal (brōō′məl) Relating to winter; wintry

brummagem (brum′ə·jəm) ☩ Making an imposing display but inferior and of little worth; showy but cheap

caducous (kə·dōō′kəs, -dyōō′-) ⚡ 1. Dropping away; falling off; deciduous

2. Fleeting; transient; unenduring

caitiff (kā′tif) ☩ Base; despicable; cowardly, wicked

calescent (kə·les′ənt) Increasing in warmth

caliginous (kə·lij′ə·nəs) Obscure; dim; misty; dark

candent (kan′dənt) Heated to whiteness; glowing

canny (kan′ē) ☆ Wary; sharp-witted; shrewd

caprylic (kə·pril′ik, ka-) ☩ Of or pertaining to an animal odor: *The caprylic scent of billygoat*

captious (kap′shəs) 1. Calculated to entrap or entangle; sophistical; tricky

2. Trivial faultfinding; carping; cavilling

carious (kār′ē·əs) Deteriorated by progressive natural changes; decayed

carking (kär′king) ☩ ⚡ Distressing; annoying; perplexing

chiastic (kī·as′tik) Characterized by an inversion of the order of words in two otherwise corresponding parallel phrases: *He went to the city, to the city went he*

chthonic (thon′ik) ✖ Dwelling or reigning in the underworld as deities or as spirits; infernal; ghostly

cinerary (sin′ə·rer″ē) Pertaining to, holding, or intended for ashes, especially those of the cremated dead

circadian (sur″kə·dē′ən) 🜔 Designating or pertaining to rhythmic biological cycles recurring approximately every twenty-four hours

cleave (klēv) 🜔 1. To adhere closely; cling; stick 2. Constant and faithful, especially as resulting from closely allied interests and affection

clubbable (klub′ə·bəl) ☆ Suitable for membership in a club; sociable

coeval (kō·ē′vəl) 🜔 Existing or occurring at the same time; contemporaneous; coetaneous

comminatory (kə·min′ə·tōr″ē, -tôr″-) Accusing publicly; denunciatory; threatening

concatenate (kon·kat′ə·nāt″) ♂ ♀ ♀ Linked together; connected

costive (kos′tiv, kô′stiv) ♆ 1. Slow or stiff in the expression of opinions and in action and reaction generally 2. Constipated

63

crabbed (krab'id, krabd) ✝ 1. Manifesting peevish, cross, or sour temper; irritable; fractious
2. Difficult to understand; abstruse; perplexing

creatic (krē·at'ik) Of or pertaining to flesh

crepuscular (kri·pus'kyə·lər) ⟩ 1. Of or like the twilight
2. Indistinct; glimmering; imperfectly luminous; obscure

cursive (kur'siv) ⚘ Of flowing writing with strokes joined and angles rounded: *Cursive script as opposed to block letters*

delitescent (del''i·tes'ənt) ⚘ 1. Latent; inactive
2. Hidden; concealed

dimidiate (di·mid'ē·āt, dī-, -it) ⚘ Divided into halves; reduced to half

dimissory (dim'i·sor''ē, -sôr''-) Granting leave to depart; dismissing

draconic (drā·kon'ik) ✝ ⟩ Of or like a dragon

dumpish (dum'pish) ✝ ⟩ 1. Dull; stupid; lethargic
2. Gloomy; melancholic; depressed

empyreal (em·pir'ē·əl, em'pə·rē-) ☆ 1. Heavenly; celestial
2. Sublime; majestic; exalted

epexegetic (ep·ek''si·jet'ik) ⟩ ↔ Providing additional explanation or clarification

epidictic (ep'i·dik'tik) ☆ ⟩ Displaying the skill of the speaker, as a dialogue or oration

eristic (e·ris'tik) ✝ ⟩ Controversial; disputatious; contentious

esculent (es'kyə·lənt) ☆ Suitable for food; edible

64

esurient (i·soor′ē·ənt) ✝ 1. Hungry; voracious; ravenous; edacious

2. Greedy; avaricious; covetous

euphuistic (yoo′fyoo·is′·tik) ✝ ♎ Displaying excessive elegance of language; high-flown and affected diction

excrescent (ik·skres′ənt) ✝ ♎ Constituting an excess; superfluous; supernumerary

exigible (ek′si·jə·bəl) ⚮ That which may be exacted or required; claimable

exoteric (ek″sə·ter′ik) 1. Easily understood; readily comprehensible

2. External; exterior; on the outside

facinorous (fə·sin′ər·əs) ✝ ♎ Extremely wicked; depraved

farctate (färk′tāt) ⚮ Full; crammed; plethoric

fatidic (fā·tid′ik, fə-) ⚮ Foretelling the future; prophetic; divinatory

feracious (fə·rā′shəs) ♎ Productive of good results; fruitful

flagitious (flə·jish′əs) ✝ ♎ Shamefully wicked; heinous; atrocious

fribble (frib′əl) ✝ Of little value or importance; trifling; paltry

frigorific (frig″ə·rif′ik) ♎ Causing or producing cold; frigiferous

froward (frō′wərd, -ərd) ✝ Perverse; willfully contrary; obstinately disobedient; refractory

frowzy (frou′zē) ✞ 🎶 1. Dirty and untidy; slovenly; slatternly; blowzy

2. Ill-smelling; musty; fusty

fructuous (fruk′choo·əs) ☆ ⟍ Productive; fruitful; profitable

frugivorous (froo·jiv′ər·əs) Fruit-eating

fugacious (fyoo·gā′shəs) 🎶 Fleeting; ephemeral; transitory; evanescent

fumacious (fyoo·mā′shəs) 🎶 Fond of smoking

funicular (fyoo·nik′yə·lər) ⟍ Pertaining to a rope or cord, or their tension

galumptious (gə·lump′shəs) ☆ ⟍ Tiptop; first-rate; superlatively good

gewgaw (gyoo′gô, goo′-) ☆ Showy but valueless; splendidly trifling

gibbous (gib′əs, jib′-) 1. Humpbacked

2. Protuberant; bulging; protruding

3. Descriptive of the moon when the illumi-nated portion is more than a semicircle but less than a circle

glyptic (glip′tik) 🎶 Of or pertaining to carving or engraving, especially on precious gems

66

gnathonic (na·thon′ik) ✝ ✖ Falsely flattering; fawning; sycophantic; parasitic

gnomic (nō′mik, nom′ik) ☆ 1. Full of aphorisms or maxims
2. Wise and pithy

gratulant (grach′ə·lənt) ☆ Expressing joy or satisfaction; congratulatory

graveolent (grə·vē′əl·ənt) ✝ 🐚 Having a rank smell; fetid; stinking

gravific (gra·vif′ik) That which makes heavy or produces weight

gregarian (gri·gār′ē·ən) Belonging to the herd or common sort

gressorial (gre·sōr′ē·əl, -sôr′-) 🐚 Adapted for walking; ambulatory

hebdomadal (heb·dom′ə·dəl) ✖ Once every seven days; weekly

hesperian (he·spēr′ē·ən) 🐚 Of the west; western; occidental

heuristic (hyoo·ris′tik) 𝔏 Helping to discover or learn; serving to indicate, point out, guide, or reveal

hiemal (hī′ə·məl) Of winter; wintry; hibernal

hieratic (hī″ə·rat′ik, hī·rat′-) Pertaining to priests or the priesthood; priestly; sacerdotal

horrisonous (hô·ris′ən·əs) ✝ ✖ Sounding very bad; horribly discordant

hortulan (ho′chə·lən) Of or belonging to a garden or gardening

hubristic (hyōō·bris′tik, hōō′bris-) ✝ Insolent; contemptuous; wantonly arrogant

hypnagogic (hip″nə·goj′ik) Inducing sleep

hypnopompic (hip″nə·pom′pik) Dispelling sleep; waking

illative (il′ə·tiv, i·lā′-) ♒ Of or concerning a word or phrase that introduces an inference, such as "therefore" or "as a consequence of "; of or forming conclusions

immanent (im′ə·nənt) Indwelling; inherent

immund (ə·mənd′) ✝ ♒ Unclean; foul; filthy

impavid (im·pav′id) ☆ Not afraid; fearless; undaunted

indehiscent (in″di·his′ənt) Not opening at maturity: *The apple is an indehiscent fruit*

irenic (ī·ren′ik, -rē′nik) ☆ Promoting peace; peaceful

irrefragable (i·ref′rə·gə·bəl) ☆ ⭦ Undeniable; indisputable; that cannot be refuted

isagogic (ī″sə·goj′ik) ⭦ Introductory

jejune (ji·jōōn′) ✝ ♒ 1. Dull; insipid; lacking interest 2. Juvenile; immature; childish

jerkwater (jurk′wô″tər, -wot″ər) ✝ ⭦ Of minor importance; insignificant: *Jerkwater bureaucrats*

labile (lā′bil) Prone to change; unstable

lethiferous (li·thif′ər·əs) ✝ ♒ ↔ That causes or results in death; deadly

lilting (lilt′ing) Gay and lively; merry and with a swing

lotic (lō′tik) Pertaining to or living in rapidly moving currents of water

luculent (lōō′kyoo·lənt) ☆ 🎵 1. Readily understood; clear; lucid
2. Convincing; cogent

macaronic (mak″ə·ron′ik) ↘ 1. Involving a mixture of languages
2. Mixed; jumbled

maculate (mak′yə·lit) ✝ 1. Spotted; blotched· stained
2. Defiled; impure

maieutic (mā·yōō′tik) 🎵 Of the Socratic method of bringing into full consciousness latent ideas or memories; intellectual midwifery

malic (mal′ik, mā′lik) Pertaining to or derived from apples

mantic (man′tik) Of the attempt to foretell the future by occult means

marcescent (mär·ses′ənt) Withering but not falling off, as parts of certain plants

marigenous (mə·rij′ə·nəs) Produced in or by the sea

matutinal (mə·tōōt′ə·nəl, -tyōōt-) 🎵 Pertaining to or occurring in the morning; early

mawkish (mô′kish) ✝ ↘ 1. Characterized by sickly, weak sentimentality
2. Lacking in robustness, strength, or vigor; insipid

melic (mel′ik) Intended to be sung; lyric

melliferous (mə·lif′ər·əs) ☆ 🎵 Yielding or producing honey

mephitic (mə·fit′ik) ☦ Bad-smelling; noxious

minatory (min′ə·tōr″ē, -tôr″-) ☦ Portending punishment; threatening; menacing

morbific (môr·bif′ik) ☦ Causing disease or sickness

mordant (môr′dənt) ☦ Biting; caustic; cutting; sarcastic

morganatic (môr″gə·nat′ik) Of a marriage between a man of high rank and a commoner

niggling (nig′ling) ☦ Petty; inconsequential: *Niggling differences in terminology*

noetic (nō·et′ik) 🛡 Of or pertaining to the mind or intellect

obstruent (ob′strōō·ənt) Producing an obstruction; hindering

oddling (od′ling) ☦ ✕ Odd and extraordinary in the sense of being lonely and queer: *Oddling crows*

omophagic (o″mə·faj′ik) ☦ ✕ Of or pertaining to eating raw flesh

oneiric (ō·nī′rik) Of or pertaining to dreams

operose (op′ə·rôs″) ☦ Involving much labor; laborious

70

opposable (ə·pō′zə·bəl) 1. Capable of being resisted, fought, or opposed

2. Capable of being placed opposite something else: *Opposable thumb*

oppugnant (ə·pug′nənt) ✝ ⚔ Opposing; antagonistic; contrary

orgulous (ôr′gyə·ləs) ✝ Proud and haughty; swelling

orotund (ōr′ə·tund″, ôr′-) 1. Full and resonant; clear and strong: said of the voice

2. Pompous; showy; bombastic: said of a style of speaking or writing

overweening (ō″vər·wē′ning) ✝ ⚔ 1. Excessively proud; arrogant; conceited: *A brash and overweening general*

2. Exaggerated; excessive: *Overweening pride*

paphian (pā′fē·ən) ♂ ♀ ♀ Pertaining to love, especially its sexual and illicit manifestations; erotic

paraenetic (par·ə·net′ik) Advisory; hortatory

pavid (pav′id) ✝ ⚔ Quaking with fear; afraid; frightened

pelagic (pə·laj′ik) 𝕌 1. Of or pertaining to the high seas; oceanic

2. Living on or near the surface of the open sea

periphrastic (per″ə·fras′tik) ✝ ↔ Using many words when few would do; verbose; roundabout; circumlocutory

perspicuous (per·spik′yōō·əs) ☆ Clearly expressed; lucid

pharisaical (far″i·sā′i·kəl) ✝ ↔ Affecting the appearance of sanctity and morality; sanctimonious

piacular (pī·ak′yə·lər) ⚔ 1. Serving to atone or make amends for; expiatory

2. Sinful; wicked

pinguescent (ping·gwes′ənt) ✝ 𝕌 Becoming fat
pinguid (ping′gwid) ✝ 𝕌 Greasy; oily; unctuous
pleonastic (plē″ə·nas′tik) ✝ Use of words superfluously; redundant

72

postprandial (pōst·pran′dē·əl) Occurring after a meal, especially dinner: *Postprandial oratory*

profluent (prof′lōō·ənt) ☆ Flowing smoothly and copiously

propaedeutic (prō″pi·dōō′tik, -dyōō-) Of or pertaining to preliminary instruction; introductory

purulent (pyoor′ə·lənt, pyoor′yə-) ✚ ♉ Of, containing, or discharging pus; suppurating: *Purulent sores*

quadrumanous (kwo·drōō′mə·nəs) ⚹ Having all four feet adapted for use as hands; four-handed

quercine (kwur′sin, -sīn) ⚹ Of or pertaining to an oak

raptorial (rap·tōr′ē·əl, -tôr′-) Given to seizing prey; predatory

rasorial (rə·sōr′ē·əl, -sôr′-) Characteristically scratching the ground for food, as poultry

refluent (ref′lōō·ənt) ♉ Flowing back; receding; ebbing

remontant (ri·mon′tənt) Flowering more than once in a season: said of certain roses

73

renitent (ri·nīt′ənt, ren′i·tənt) ☦ Resisting or opposing stubbornly; recalcitrant

sabulous (sab′yə·ləs) Sandy; gritty; arenaceous

sapid (sap′id, -īd) ☆ Flavorsome; savory; palatable

scacchic (ska′kik) ⊻ Pertaining to or like chess

scribacious (skri·bā′shəs) ⊻ Given to or fond of writing

scrofulous (skrof′yə·ləs) ☦ Morally corrupt; degenerate

semiotic (sē″mē·ot′ik, -mī-) Of or pertaining to signs or symptoms

sempiternal (sem″pi·tur′nəl) ☆ ⚲ Enduring constantly; everlasting; eternal

sequacious (si·kwā′shəs) ☦ ⚲ Given to the slavish or unreasoning serving or following of others

seraphic (si·raf′ik) ☆ Of or like an angel; angelic

serried (ser′ēd) Pressed closely together; in closely packed ranks: *Dark columns of serried clouds*

spumescent (spyoo·mes′ənt) ⚲ Of, like, or having the appearance of froth or foam

strepitous (strep′i·təs) ⊻ Making a great clamor; noisy; boisterous

succose (sə′kōs) ⊻ Full of juice or sap; juicy; succulent

suctorial (suk·tōr′ē·əl, -tôr′-) Adapted for sucking or suction: *The squid's suctorial arms*

supernal (soo·pur′nəl) ☆ 1. Existing or dwelling in the heavens; heavenly; divine
2. Lofty; sublime; elevated

supine (soo·pīn′) 1. Mentally inactive, inert, or indolent; sluggish; listless
2. Lying on one's back, face up

74

suppositive (sə·poz′i·tiv) Based upon or involving theory, hypothesis, or supposition; conjectural

tabescent (tə·bes′ənt) ✝ Wasting away; withering; emaciating

tectonic (tek·ton′ik) 🎺 1. Of or pertaining to building or construction
2. Of or pertaining to the structure of the earth's crust

thalassic (thə·las′ik) 🎺 1. Of or pertaining to bays, gulfs, and smaller or inland seas as distinguished from large oceanic bodies
2. Growing, living, or found in the sea

thetical (thet′ə·kəl) Set forth positively or absolutely; involving positive, prescribed statement

theurgic (thē·ur′jik) 🎺 1. Relating to supposedly divine intervention in human affairs
2. Magical

thewless (thyoo′lis) ✝ 1. Lacking bodily strength; without vigor or spirit
2. Cowardly; timid

titubant (tich′oo·bənt) ✝ Staggering; tottering; reeling; unsteady

totipalmate (tō″tə·pal′mit, -māt) Having all toes fully webbed

tramontane (trə·mon′tān) 🎺 1. Dwelling or situated beyond mountains
2. Foreign and barbarous

75

transcalent (trans·kā′lənt) Freely transmitting heat; pervious to heat; diathermanous

turgescent (tur·jes′ənt)  Becoming swollen; swelling

umbrageous (um·brā′jəs) 1. Creating or providing shade; shady

2. Easily offended; inclined to take umbrage for little cause

untoward (un·tōrd′, -tôrd′) ✝ 1. Unfavorable; unfortunate

2. Hard to deal with; intractable; perverse

unwonted (un·wōn′tid, -wôn′-) Not customary or habitual; unusual

uranic (yoo·ran′ik) Of or having to do with the heavens; celestial

vaticinal (və·tis′ə·nəl) Characterized by prophesy; prophetic

venatic (vē·nat′ik) Of or pertaining to hunting

verecund (ver′ə·kund″) 🎵 Bashful; modest; shy

vespertine (ves′pər·tin, -tīn″) 🎵 Of, occurring in, or pertaining to the evening

vestiary (ves′tē·er″ē) Of or pertaining to garments or dress; of clothes or vestments

viatic (vī·at′ik) ↖ Of a road, journey, or travel

vicenary (vis′ə·ner″ē) ↖ Pertaining to or consisting of twenty

vicinal (vis′ə·nəl) 🎵 Neighboring; adjacent; bordering

villatic (vi·lat′ik) Of or pertaining to the country or to a farm; rural

volant (vō′lənt) 1. Flying, or capable of flying 2. Moving lightly; nimble; agile

wonted (wōn′tid, wôn′-) Customary; habitual; usual

77

N<small>ON-VERBAL</small> <small>TESTS INDICATE THAT</small> speakers of English notice and remember colors for which they know a name more readily than those for which they have to concoct a description (yellowish orange or bluish gray). Thus, if gamboge, griseous, and the rest are added to your frame of color reference, your *perception*, as well as your speech, will be more vivid and precise.

Six

Shades of Meaning

FROM BLACK . . .

swarthy (swôr'<u>th</u>ē, -<u>th</u>ē̠)   blackish; dark and dusky

fuliginous (fyo͞o·lij'ə·nəs)   sooty; dull dark gray

fuscous (fus'kəs)   dark and somber brownish gray

adust (ə·dust')   scorched or burn-darkened brown

carbuncle (kär'bung·kəl)   dark grayish; red-brown

cupreous (kyo͞o'prē·əs, ko͞o'-)   metallic reddish brown; copper-colored

sepia (sē'pē·ə)   dark reddish brown

roan (rōn)   reddish brown; chestnut-colored

rubiginous (ro͞o·bij'ə·nəs)   reddish brown; rust-colored

russet (rus'it)   reddish brown

bay (bā)   reddish brown

sorrel (sôr'əl, sor'-)   light reddish brown

terra cotta (ter'ə kot'ə)   brownish orange

tawny (tô'nē)   dark or dull yellowish brown

79

sienna (sē·en′ə) yellowish brown

buff (buf) yellowish brown; medium or dark tan

bisque (bisk) ♀ light grayish brown; beige; other synonyms from the lavender worlds of fashion and interior decoration: almond, putty, bone, malt, oatmeal, shell, and hot sand

dun (dun) dull grayish brown; dust-colored

cyaneous (sī·an′ē·əs) deep blue

perse (purs) deep grayish blue

livid (liv′id) dull grayish blue

gridelin (grid′ə·lən, -lin) grayish violet

azure (azh′ər, ā′zhər) light purplish blue; sky blue; cerulean

celestine (sel′i·stīn″, si·les′tin) pale blue; sky-colored

purpure (pur′pyoor) purple

tyrian (tir′ē·ən) rich purple

puce (pyo͞os) brownish purple

heliotrope (hē′lē·ə·trōp′, hēl′yə-) ♀ light purple; reddish lavender

violescent (vī″ə·les′ent) bluish purple

mauve (mōv) pale bluish purple

testaceous (te·stā′shəs) brownish red; brick red

rufous (ro͞o′fəs) brownish red

rubious (ro͞o′bē·əs) deep red; ruddy-colored

cerise (sə·rēs′, -rēz′) bright clear red; cherry red

carmine (kär′min, -mīn) deep purplish red; crimson

murrey (mur′ē) dark purplish red

fuchsia (fyo͞o′shə) bright purplish red

magenta (mə·jen′tə) purplish red

amaranthine (am″ə·ran′thin) purplish red

vinaceous (vī·nā′shəs) the color of red wine

rubicund (ro͞o′·bə·kund″) reddish

80

damask (dam′əsk) deep pink

incarnadine (in·kär′nə·dīn″) pale red or pink; flesh-colored (Caucasian)

virescent (vī·res′ənt) slightly greenish; turning or becoming green; viridescent

verdure (vur′jər) greenish; the fresh green color of growing things

patina (pat′ən·ə) rusty green color, as on surface of old bronze

verdigris (vur·də·grēs′, -gris′) blue-green color, as on copper, brass, or bronze surfaces exposed to the atmosphere

viridian (və·rid′ē·ən) bluish green

glaucous (glô′kəs) green with grayish blue cast; sea green

berylline (ber′ə·lin′, -līn′) pale sea green

xanthous (zan′thəs) yellow

jaundiced (jôn′dist, jän′-) yellowish

primrose (prim′rōz″) pale yellow

fallow (fal′ō) pale brownish yellow

canary (kə·nār′ē) light clear yellow

fulvous (ful′vəs) dull yellowish gray

coralline (kôr′ə·lin, -lin″, kor′-) pinkish yellow

saffron (saf′rən) orange-yellow

gamboge (gam·bōj′, -boozh′) bright yellow with slight orange cast

orpiment (ôr′pə·mənt) gold; king's yellow

aureate (ôr′ē·it, -āt″) golden yellow

griseous (gris′ē·əs, griz′-) bluish gray; pearl gray

grizzly (griz′lē) grayish

hoary (hōr′ē, hôr′ē) grayish white, as with age

cadaverous (kə·dav′ər·əs) whitish; pale, pallid, and wan

ashen (ash'ən) extremely pale; ash-colored
albescent (al·bes'ənt) becoming white; whitish
niveous (niv'ē·əs) snow white
argent (är'jənt) silvery white

... TO WHITE

HARLEQUIN

variegated (vār'ə·gā"tid) marked with patches or
   spots of different colors
piebald (pī'bôld") having patches of black and
   white or, less frequently, other colors
mottled (mot'əld) spotted or blotched in coloring,
   as marble; dappled
punctate (pungk'tāt) marked with dots or tiny
   spots; spotted
brindled (brin'dəld) streaked or spotted with a
   darker color
harlequin (här'lə·kwin, -kin) of many colors; parti-
   colored
tabby (tab'ē) brown or gray and marked with darker parallel stripes or streaks

82

RHADAMANTHUS, SON OF ZEUS AND one of the judges of the underworld, was renouned for his exemplary justice. The word *rhadamanthine* preserves this relic of ancient wisdom, and means strictly and inflexibly just. In like manner, the words that comprise this chapter derive from actual, fictional, or mythical proper names (with few exceptions) and embody uncommon and often transporting allusions.

Seven

Esoterica

aesculapian (es″kyǝ·lā′pē·ǝn) ⚕ ↔ Relating to that which is medical or to the art of healing. From Aesculapius, the Roman god of medicine

amaranthine (am″ǝ·ran′thin, -thīn) ☆ ⚕ ↔ Undying or having no end; immortal. From the Amaranth, imaginary never-fading flower

ananias (an′ǝ·nī′ǝs) ✝ ⚕ A teller of untruths; liar. From a follower of the apostles who was struck dead for lying

arcadian (är·kā′dē·ǝn) ☆ ⚕ Ideally simple and contented. From Arcadia, the mountain district in ancient Greece whose inhabitants lived quiet, pleasant lives

attic (at′ik) ☆ Displaying simple and refined elegance; tastefully pure; classical. Resembling the symmetry and refinement of Attica in ancient Greece

augean (ô·jē′ən) ✝ Filthy and difficult to clean; requiring hard work. From the stables of Augeas, not cleaned for thirty years

belletristic (bel″li·tris′tik) ☆ Of or concerned with belles-lettres (fine literature)

billingsgate (bil′ingz·gāt″) ✝ Coarse, abusive, and vulgar language. From a London fish market notorious for bad language

buncombe (bung′kəm) ✝ Empty, insincere speechmaking. From the name of a county in North Carolina. During the 16th Congress, the member from this district, when urged to desist from speaking, declared that he was bound to make a speech for Buncombe

cimmerian (si·mēr′ē·ən) 𝄢 Shrouded in gloom or darkness, like a mythical people said by Homer to dwell in an obscure, umbrageous mist

croesus (krē′səs) A man of great wealth. From a very wealthy king of ancient Lydia

distaff (dis′taf, -täf) ♀ Woman's work or domain; characteristic of or suitable for women. From the staff that holds wool or flax for hand-spinning

draconian (drā·kō′nē·ən) ✝ ↘ Barbarously harsh; inhumanly severe; cruel. From or characteristic

84

of Draco, chief magistrate of Athens in 621 B.C., or the severe code of laws said to have been established by him

fescennine (fes′ə·nīn″, -nin) ✝ ⚥ Obscene; lewd; licentious; scurrilous. From Fescennia in Etruria, famous for a sort of jeering dialogue in verse

gorgon (gor′gən) ✝ ♀ Exceedingly ugly or repellent woman. From one of the three winged sisters of mythology who had snakes for hair and whose looks turned beholders to stone

hecatomb (hek′ə·tōm″-tōōm″) ✝ ⚔ A large-scale slaughter or sacrifice. From the Greek ritual-slaughter of 100 oxen

janissaries (jan′i·ser″ēz) 1. Turkish infantrymen constituting the sultan's guard
2. Soldiers generally, especially as instruments of tyranny

jehu (jē′hyōō) ✝ A fast and reckless driver. From a king of Israel noted for his furious chariot attacks

jeremiad (jer″ə·mī′ad) ⚥ A writing or speech in a strain of grief or distress; a lamentation. Resembling the lamentations of the prophet Jeremiah

katabasis (kə·tab′ə·sis) ⚔ 1. A going down; descent
2. A retreat, especially a military retreat. From the retreat of 10,000 Greeks under Xenophon

laodicean (lā·od″ i·sē′ən, lā″ə·di·sē′ən) ✝ 𝕚 1. Lacking religious fervor, like the Christians of Laodicea

2. Lacking strong feeling generally; indifferent

mammon (mam′ən) ✝ Riches or wealth personified as an evil object of worship or greedy pursuit. From the Aramaic word for "riches" occurring in the Greek text of Matthew 6:24 and Luke 16:9–13

moloch (mō′lək) ✝ A system or method that requires frightful sacrifice. From a Canaanite idol to whom human sacrifices were made

panjandrum (pan·jan′drəm) ✝ A self-important local official; pompous minor magnate; from the burlesque title of an imaginary personage in some nonsense lines by Samuel Foote, English playwright

pasquinade (pas″kwə·nād′) 𝕚 A lampoon or satire posted in a public place. From a mutilated piece of statuary disinterred at Rome in 1501 and set up near the Piazza Navona. It became the annual custom on St. Mark's day to "restore" the torso with clothes and slogans

pinchbeck (pinch′bek″) ✝ Sham or spurious; false. After Christopher Pinchbeck, a watch and toymaker from London. He used an alloy of five parts copper and one part zinc to simulate gold

procrustean (prō·krus′tē·ən) ✝ Aiming or tending to produce uniformity by violent and arbitrary means. From the robber Procrustes, who fitted his victims to a bed by stretching or mutilating them

pukka (puk′ə) ☆ Reliable; good; genuine; first-rate. From the Hindi word *pakka* meaning cooked, ripe, or mature

86

rhadamanthine (rad″ə·man′<u>thin</u>) ☆ ↔ Strictly and inflexibly honest and just. From Rhadamanthus, son of Zeus and one of the judges of the underworld, who was renowned for his exemplary justice

rodomontade (rod″ə·mon·tād′, rō″də-) Arrogant boasting; pretentious blustering, ranting, or bragging. From Rodomonte, the boastful Saracen leader in Ariosto's *Orlando Furioso*

sardanapalian (sär″də·nə·pāl′yən) ⚜ ↔ ♀ Luxuriously effeminate. From Sardanapalus, the last king of Nineveh

saturnalia (sat″ər·nā′lē·ə, -nal′yə) Period of unrestrained license and orgiastic revelry. Derived from Roman antiquity when the festival of Saturn, held in mid-December, was observed with general unrestrained merrymaking

sibylline (sib′ə·lēn″, -līn″) ⚲ Oracular; prophetic; mysterious. Pertaining to or characteristic of the Sibyls, women of antiquity reputed to possess powers of prophecy and divination

simony (sī′mə·nē, sim′ə-) Buying, selling, or otherwise making a profit from sacred or spiritual things. From the name of Simon Magus, in allusion to his offer of money to the apostles, Acts 8:18–19

sisyphean (sis″ə·fē′ən) ⚜ ⚲ Endless, unavailing, and fruitless labor. From Sisyphus, King of Corinth, whose punishment in Hades was to roll a heavy stone up a hill; as he reached a point near the top, the stone would tumble back down the hill

solon (sō'lən) ☆ Sage; wise lawgiver; man of great knowledge. From the early Athenian legislator Solon, one of the seven sages of Greece

stakhanovite (stə·kä'nə·vīt'', -kan'ə-) ☆ ↔ 1. A Russian worker who regularly surpasses his production quota and is specially rewarded 2. A good and diligent worker

thersitical (thər·sit'i·kəl) ✝ Loud and grossly abusive foulmouthed, scurrilous. From Thersites, an ill-tongued Greek at the siege of Troy

thrasonical (thrā·son'i·kəl) ✝ Given to or marked by boasting and bragging. From a braggart soldier in Terrence's *Eunuchus*

tohu-bohu (tō'hoo·bō'hoo) ✝ ⟲ Utter confusion, disorder, and chaos. From the Hebrew words *thohu wa-bhohu,* meaning emptiness and desolation

SOONER OR LATER EVERYONE GETS A little bored with the humdrum, cliché-ridden slang we hear every day and wants to proceed, even if only for a moment, in a rather more augustan manner.

Eight

Sesquipeds

The "big words" that follow can help you. All are rated ↔ . They are more difficult to use than shorter words, and they can get you into more difficulty . . . but then, more things can go wrong with boeuf bourguignon than with hamburger.

Try their frothy rumble out on your friends . . . and enemies. Indeed, the next time you're in a fishmarket and the little man with the cigarette behind his ear says, "Hey, bub, ya want some scrod?" tell him, "No . . . you can keep your scrod . . . but have you any humuhumunukunukuapuaa?" (For correct pronunciation, consult your old Arthur Godfrey records.) If you are spared an indelicate recommendation, it will do your heart good.

One final caveat: Not everyone has read this book. The most common method of acquiring a large vocabulary is still by marrying it. Thus, if through too frequent use of these gems your meaning becomes obfuscated, your friends may wonder less what the hell you mean than who the hell you think you are.

abecedarian (ā″bē·sē·dâr′ē·ən) ✝ 1. Simple; elementary; rudimentary; introductory: *Abecedarian legal maxims*
2. Alphabetical: *Abecedarian pagination*

89

allagrugous (a″la·groo′jəs) ✟ ☿ Grim and ghastly (generally used to describe men). Source according to Jamieson's Scottish Dictionary: "moesogothic as preserved in the Uphilas version of the gospels": *A treacherous cabal of allagrugous characters*

animadversion (an″ə·mad·vur′zhən) ✟ A censorious comment or adverse remark; criticism

antephialtic (an″tē·fē·al′tik) Preventive of nightmares: *An antephialtic potion*

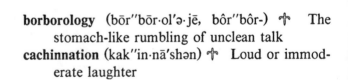

autochthonous (ô·tok′thə·nəs) 1. Relating to the original or earliest inhabitants of a region, their effects, or their time; aboriginal: *Fossil remains of a forgotten and autochthonous people*
2. Not foreign; indigenous; endemic; native: *A fleshy specimen of autochthonous breadfruit*

bandersnatch (ban′dər·snach″) ✟ 1. Imaginary wild animal of fierce disposition
2. An uncouth or unconventional person, especially one deemed a menace or nuisance

borborology (bōr″bōr·ol′ə·jē, bôr″bôr-) ✟ The stomach-like rumbling of unclean talk

cachinnation (kak″in·nā′shən) ✟ Loud or immoderate laughter

convallariaceous (kən"və·lār"ē·ā'shəs) The aspidistra, a lily; of or like it (poetic)

defenestration (dē·fen"i·strā'shən) The act of throwing a thing or person out of a window

filipendulous (fil"ə·pen'jə·ləs, -də·ləs) Hanging by a thread or string: *Filipendulous apples, ripe and ready to fall*

floccilation (flok"sə·lā'shən) Searching for imaginary objects, or picking of the bedclothes by a delirious patient

floccinaucinihilipilification (good luck) The action or process of estimating a thing, idea, etc., as worthless. The longest word in the *Oxford English Dictionary*

furfuraceous (fur"fyoo·rā'shəs) ✟ 1. Scaly; branlike; scurfy: *Furfuraceous skin is a symptom of psoriasis*
2. Covered with dandruff: *A furfuraceous scalp*

inexpugnable (in"ik·spug'nə·bəl) ☆ That cannot be taken by assault or storm; unconquerable; impregnable: *An inexpugnable medieval fortress*

infralapsarianism (good luck) The doctrine that God foresaw and permitted the fall of man from grace and that His plan of salvation for some people followed and was a consequence of the fall

ioblepharous (ī·ə·ble'fär·əs) Violet-lidded; describing the presence of coloring on the eyelids of a female person or statue: *Ioblepharous caryatids majestically adorn the Acropolis*

irrefrangible (ir"i·fran'jə·bəl) That cannot or should not be broken; inviolable: *Irrefrangible rules of etiquette*

91

latitudinarian (lat"i·to͞od"ə·nâr'ē·ən, -tyo͞od"-) ☆
Characterized by liberality in opinion or action;
tolerant in one's views: *Slow to criticize or con-
demn, he is admired for his latitudinarian ways*

omphaloskepsis (om"fə·lō·skep'sis) Contemplation
of the navel for the purpose of attaining philo-
sophic calm

**osseocarnisanguineoviscericartilaginonervomedul-
lary** (good luck) The structure of the human
body, coined by Thomas Love Peacock in
Headlong Hall

philotheoparoptesism (good luck) The process of
slowly cooking those who have suffered the
church's displeasure. From the word roots
meaning "for the love of God" and "roasting
by a slow fire." Coined by Thomas Love Peacock in *Maid Marian*

pneumonoultramicroscopicsilicovolcanoconiosis
(good luck) A lung disease caused by inhaling
dust-like silicon and volcanic ash particles so
exceedingly minute as to be seen only with a
microscope

polychrestic (pol"ē·krest'ik) Serving and adapted
for several different uses: *An ingenious and
polychrestic invention*

psittacistic (sit"ə·siz'tik) ✝ Speaking in a mechanical, repetitive, and meaningless way: *The old
professor was a boring and psittacistic speaker.*
From the root meaning "parrot," as in psittaco-
sis (parrot fever)

rhyparography (rī" pə·rog'rə·fe) ✝ The printing or
painting of sordid and filthy pictures

sanguisugent (sang·gwi′sə·gənt) ✝ Bloodsucking: *A slimy, sanguisugent leech*

sedentarize (sed·ən′tə·rīz) To take up, or cause to take up, a permanent residence after a life of nomadic wandering: *The valley's verdant lure sedentarized the nomads*

septentrional (sep·ten′trē·ə·nəl) Belonging to the north; northern: *Septentrional winds*

stultiloquence (stul·təl′ə·kwəns) ✝ Foolish or senseless talk; babble; twaddle

synergistic (sin″ər·jis′tik) ☆ Working together; cooperating: *Synergistic muscles*

temerarious (tem″ə·rār′ē·əs) ✝ Reckless; heedless; rash: *One usually regrets his hasty and temerarious remarks*

thaumaturgic (thô″mə·tur′jik) Of or involving the supposed working of miracles; magical: *Mysterious choruses of thaumaturgic incantations*

triskaidekaphobia (tri″skə·dekə·fō′bē·ə) Fear of the number 13 or Friday the 13th

ultracrepidarian (ul·trə·kre·pə·dâr′ē·ən) ✝ Going beyond one's province; a person who does this, especially an ignorant or presumptuous critic

SEVERAL YEARS AGO, WHILE WALKING along New Orleans' Dryades Street one mild evening, I witnessed an instructive exchange. A lithe and venturesome man, in his early twenties, was pulling himself onto the small elevated rear porch of a rickety antebellum house. As he edged over the wooden railing, he gazed into what must have been an invitingly open window toward an unmistakable armful of real womanhood, and asked:-

Nine

Words
of Whimsey

> "Where ya at, ya mother?"
>   "Awl rye [all right]," she replied.
> "Where ya mother at?"
>   "Long gone," she answered.

End of conversation. Exeunt both parties into the bedroom.

The moral of this story is that you can never tell where or when you will encounter an unusual usage of a commonplace word. Man seems to have a compelling urge to play with sounds, to repeat them (reduplication), imitate them (onomatopoeia), blend them (portmanteau words), and make puns of them. This chapter presents some of the most original and amusing examples of the above currently in use. Consider the rhythmic lilt of *hokeypokey,* the perfect aptness of *galumph* (marching along heavily or clumsily), and the pretentious punstering of *bustluscious.* They and the rest remind us that words are not hardened dictionary definitions but fluid thoughts, made audible.

95

bustluscious (bust·lush′əs) ☆ ♛ ♀ Having or characterized by shapely mammalia, usually of substantial size; stacked. A pun on "mudluscious," by E. E. Cummings

carbecue (kär′bə·kyo͞o″) ♛ A large oven for melting away unsalvageable material from a junked car, which is rotated on a spit

comitology (kə″mit·ol′ə·jē) The study of the committee as a phenomenon

dontopedalogy (don·tə·ped·al′ə·jē) ♱ The aptitude for putting one's foot in one's mouth. Coined by Prince Philip of Great Britain unwittingly for Spiro Agnew

erectarine (i·rek′t̸ə·rēn″) ♛ A rhythm instrument consisting of a mopstick with bottle caps attached

galumph (gə·lumf′) ♱ ✼ 1. To move or march along heavily or clumsily. Coined in *Through the Looking Glass* by Lewis Carroll: *Spent of all his energy he went galumphing home*
2. To prance in a self-satisfied, triumphant manner: *A playful, gracefully galumphing, and most affectionate monster*

gawkocracy (gôk·ok′rə·sē) ♱ ✼ Persons who watch television

gobbledygook (gob″əl·dē·gook′) ♱ ✼ Derisive term for the mystifying and stilted language of official documents and communications. Also called *bafflegab* and *officialese*

gongoozler (gon·go͞oz′lər) ♱ An inquisitive idler who stares and gawks for prolonged periods at anything out of the ordinary

96

hoity-toity (hoi′tē·toi′tē) ✝ 1. Flighty; giddy; frolic-
some

2. Peevish; huffy; petulant

hokeypokey (hō′kē·pō′kē) ✝ Trickery; deception;
hocus-pocus

moondoggle (mōōn′dog″əl) ✝ Useless exploration
of the moon that is wasteful of time and money.
From the word *boondoggle*

ostrobogulous (os·trə·bog′yə·ləs) ✝ ↔ A vehement
oath of expansive meaning. In response to an
accusation that he had been turned into a
dromedary, Victor Newburg declared the story:
ostrobogulous piffle

scungilaginous (skun·ji·la′jə·nəs) 🔔 ↔ ♂ Of the
semifluid gelatinous consistency of male geni-
talia. Probably from the Italian word *scungilli*.
meaning conch

snollygoster (snol′ē·gos″tər) ✝ 🔔 A clever, shrewd,
but unscrupulous person. Probably from *snal-
lygaster,* a mythical creature that preys on poultry and children

stagorium (sta·gôr′ē·um) An establishment (bar or
resort hotel) that serves as a meeting place for
unmarrieds

97

ufologist (yo͞o·fol'ə·jist) One who is interested in unidentified flying objects. From the initials U.F.O.

wazoo (wä'zo͞o) 🎵 A generic term for the human fundament and/or pudenda: *How's your old wazoo?*

ENGLISH HAS CHANGED SO RAPIDLY in the last 1500 years that no modern speaker can comprehend Anglo-Saxon without first studying it almost as a foreign language. Fortunately, the changes have been mostly for the better; of the approximately 125 major world languages (those spoken by more than one million persons each), English is generally thought to have the most prodigious vocabulary and thus most susceptible of precise and subtle differentiation.

en

Wordmaking

The reasons for this comprehensiveness and agility derive largely from the ease by which new English words may be formulated. There are four chief ways to do so: give new meaning to an existing word, borrow a term from a foreign language, make up an entirely new word out of the blue, or combine two or more existing words or word elements.

Putting new meaning into old words is much like putting new wine into old bottles: something of the old flavor usually filters through. The new meanings do not necessarily, nor even usually, obliterate the old ones; rather, they exist concomitantly. The word *set,* for instance, has more than 100 distinct meanings. It is rare only in the extent, not in the fact, of its duplicity. Indeed, if you thumb through your dictionary, you will see that the great majority of our words have been metaphorized, the bulk of them more than once.

A second technique of word-formation—borrowing —comes naturally, for in language as in all things, we evince a marked propensity toward sloth. Since it is often easier to import a word from another language or dialect than to summon the creative effort to make an entirely new one (or even re-make an existing one), we do so with great frequency. *Spaghetti* and *hors d'oeuvre* are perfect examples of this; likewise *woodchuck* (from the Algonquin Indians) and *gnu* (from the African Hottentots).

Original contributions to our stock of words are rare. The few that we find are mostly the result of man's childlike inclination to play with sounds . . . often by imitating and repeating them. Shakespeare, for instance, coined *honorificabilitudinitatibus*, meaning nothing (but having general reference to word-swallowing pedantry) in *Love's Labour's Lost*. A few hundred years later, Edward Kasner, an American mathematician, reputedly asked his nine-year-old nephew if he could think of a word that would signify the number 1 followed by 100 zeroes. The boy, we are told, promptly replied: *googol*, as good a word as any. You will find it in your dictionary. But perhaps the best examples of all are found in *Through the Looking Glass* by Lewis Carroll:

> He took his vorpal sword in hand:
>   Long time the manxome foe he sought—
> So rested he by the Tumtum tree,
>   And stood a while in thought.
>
> And as in uffish thought he stood
>   The Jabberwock, with eyes of flame,
> Came whiffling through the tulgey wood,
>   And burbled as it came.

100

Combination is a fourth method of word-formation, and likely the one you are most familiar with. It encompasses attaching one distinct word to another, blending the sounds of separate words, and pulling together word elements (roots, prefixes, and suffixes). *Blackbird, bunkhouse, bumblebee, brainwash, whatnot, whatsoever*—there are thousands more—are a few examples of attachment without modification. In contrast, the formation of blends, also known as portmanteau words, requires that two distinct sounds be combined into a third. For instance, *motel* is the blend of "motor" and "hotel", *brunch* of "breakfast" and "lunch", and *flush* of "flash" and "blush." The third form of combination, that of uniting roots with prefixes and suffixes, is the most challenging of all. Each of the thousands of identifiable elements always has essentially the same significance, regardless of the manner in which it is combined. Thus, any person familiar with their use can create virtually endless numbers of new words. Toward encouraging and facilitating this end, there follows a listing of some of the most frequently used roots, prefixes, and suffixes. But first, some words about their use.

Roots carry more weight in determining a word's significance than prefixes or suffixes; roots are the primary determiners of meaning. A single word may have two, three, or more of them; if so, they are of equal importance. Unlike prefixes and suffixes—which, by definition, come either at the beginnings or ends of words, respectively—roots shift their positions. Many words do not actually have the roots they appear to contain ... there are many coincidences of spelling. Lastly, one should recall that words are constantly in a state of flux and transition. New meanings often overshadow and replace the old, so that the current meaning of any word might well have no logical connection with the original sense of the root. (This is not important for making words of your own, but for understanding all the others.)

Both prefixes and suffixes modify the root. The suffix, however, has a much smaller role than the prefix in influencing the meaning of the word; its primary task is to identify the word as a noun, verb, adjective, or adverb. Finally, when the prefix ends in a consonant different from the initial letter of the root, it usually changes its terminal consonant to match the root.

ROOTS

(ALPHABETIZED BY MEANING)

❁

ROOT	*MEANING*	*ROOT*	*MEANING*
pan .... omni	all	fer	bring, bear, yield
		voc	call
arch	ancient	port .... lat	carry
zo	animal		
rog .... rogat	ask	fortuna	chance
		ped	child
cred	believe	chrom	color
flect .... flex	bend	vinc .... vict	conquer
test	to bear witness		
hem .... hemato	blood	crea	create
		cise	cut
nasc .... nat	to be born, to spring forth	mort .... mors necr	death
bibl	book		

ROOT	MEANING	ROOT	MEANING
claim .... clam	declare, call out, cry out	cor .... cord cour	heart
hetero	different	grav ....,	heavy
pel .... puls	drive, push, throw	ten .... tain tent	hold together, hold
vac	empty	sacer .... sacr hiero sanct	holy
iso	equal		
phobe.......... phobia	fear, hatred	cide	kill
prim .... prime	first	mega	large
		ultima	last
flu .... flux	flow	ridi .... risi	laughter
sequ	follow	leg .... jus jur nom	law
liber .... liver	free		
theo	god	duc............. duct duce	lead
magna	great		
medi	half, middle, between	bio .... viv vivi vita	life
man .... manu	by hand		
pen .... pend pens	hang	lus............. lum luc photo	light
eu	happy, pleasing		
capit	head		
iatr	healing		
aud............. aus	hear, listen	min	little

103

ROOT	MEANING	ROOT	MEANING
philo	love	mem	remember
phile		simil	resembling
phila		arch	ruler, leader
amic		homo	same
anthrop	man		
poly	many	mar	sea
multi		mer	
fac	make	vis	see
fact		vid	
fic		scope	
fect		auto	self
meter	measure	mitt	send
psych	mind, soul	miss	
mob	move	ac	sharp
mot		acr	
mov		brev	short
nov	new	clud	shut
neo		clus	
neg	not, deny	dorm	sleep
uni	one	micro	small
alter	other	aster	star
ali		astro	
idio	peculiar	rect	straight, right
pop	people	recti	
dem		forc	strong
demo		fort	
lic	permit	path	suffering, feeling
licit		cap	take, receive
poten	power	cep	
posse		cept	
potes			

ROOT	MEANING	ROOT	MEANING
put	think	gyn	woman
chron tempo tempor	time	logo	word
dent dont	tooth	opus oper	work
ver veri	true	graph scrib scrip	write
feder fide feal fid	trust, faith	mis miso	wrong, bad, hate
cosm	universe, order	anni annu enni	year
migra	wander		
hydro aqu	water	ced cede ceed cess	yield, surrender, go
endo	within		

PREFIXES

(ALPHABETIZED BY MEANING)

❀

PREFIX	MEANING	PREFIX	MEANING
amb- ambi-	about, both, around	post-	after
		palim-	again
super- hyper-	above, beyond	omni- pan-	all
an-	absence of, not		
tra- trans-	across, through, over	circ- circum- peri-	around

PREFIX	MEANING	PREFIX	MEANING
a- .... at, in, on, to		pent- .... five	
ab- .... away, from abs- de- apo-		penta- quin- quint- quinque-	
		pro- .... forward, forth	
re- .... back, again ana-		tetr- .... four	
mal- .... bad, evil		tetra- quad- quadr- quadri-	
ante- .... before pre- fore- pro-		quartet- .... fourth	
		off- .... from	
infra- .... below		bene- .... good, well	
para- .... beside, position		hemi- .... half	
inter- .... between, among		demi- semi-	
ultra- .... beyond extra- trans-		crypto- .... hidden	
cata- .... down de-		cent- .... hundred centi- hecto-	
oct- .... eight octa- octo-		en- .... in, into em- in- im-	
equi- .... equal		intro-	
pseudo- .... false		be- .... intensive	
prim- .... first prot- proto-		macro- .... large	

106

PREFIX	MEANING	PREFIX	MEANING
poly-	many	hept-	seven
mult-		hepta-	
multi-		sept-	
		septe-	
neo-	new	septem-	
		septi-	
nona-	nine	hex-	six
novem-		hexa-	
ennea-		sex-	
in-	not	dis-	take away, deprive of
un-			
im-		deca-	ten
il-		deka-	
ir-		deci-	
non-			
a-		kilo-	thousand
nil-	nothing	mill-	
		milli-	
paleo-	old, ancient	tri-	three
mon-	one	per-	through
mono-		dia-	
uni-			
		ad-	to, toward
e-	out, from	com-	together, with
ex-			
ec-		di-	two, double, separate
ef-		amphi-	
super-	over, above, greater in quantity	bi-	twice
supr-		bin-	
sur-		bis-	
hyper-			
vic-	in place of	sub-	under, beneath
vice-		hypo-	

107

PREFIX	MEANING	PREFIX	MEANING
epi-	upon, beside, among	eu-	well
		holo-	wholly, entire

SUFFIXES

(ALPHABETIZED BY MEANING)

❁

NOUN SUFFIX	MEANING	NOUN SUFFIX	MEANING
-ion -sion -tion -age -ness -ment -ure -ity -iety -ty -ence -ency -ance -ancy -tude -hood -ture	act of, state of, result of	-ic -ine	nature of, like
		-dom -ship	office, state, skill, dignity, profession
		-eer -ster -ant -ent	doer of an action
		-ary -ery -ory	relation to, place where
-ate	cause, make	-ette -let -ling -ule -kin -cule -icle	very small, diminutive
-art -ard	derogatory agency		
-ism	doctrine, condition, system, act	-y	inclined to, tend to
-ine -stress -trix -ess	feminine agency or condition	**ADJECTIVE SUFFIX**	**MEANING**
		-ive	causing, making

108

ADJECTIVE SUFFIX	MEANING
-ful	full of
-ous	
-some	having
-oid	like, resemblance
-ine	
-esque	
-en	made of, make
-an	native of,
-ian	relating to
-ish	origin, nature, resembling
-ite	quality of, mineral product
-al	relating to
-less	without

VERB SUFFIX	MEANING
-ate	to make
-en	
-esce	
-fy	
-ize	

ADVERB SUFFIX	MEANING
-wards	direction
-ly	like, manner of
-wise	manner, in the style of

VARIED SUFFIX	MEANING
-able	able to, can do
-ible	
-osis	action, process
-esis	
-asis	
-post	after, following
-ar	one who, that which
-er	
-or	
-ist	
-ile	relating to, suitable for, capable of

❀

Pronunciation Guide/Vocabulary Test

"SHADES OF MEANING " HAVE BEEN EXCLUDED HERE IN THE interest of providing an accurate and challenging vocabulary test. To take the test, simply cover the "correct answers" column with a piece of paper, and proceed. You might try testing yourself before reading this book and then afterward. Any segment of 50 or 100 words will provide you with an accurate bellwether of your accomplishment, so you need not take the entire test. Do not be discouraged if you do poorly: No vocabulary test anywhere is more difficult than the one that follows. If you answer 25% correctly, without guessing wildly, you are doing better than most college graduates. If you are correct 50% of the time, you are doing better than most intelligent college graduates (an important distinction). Should you answer 75% correctly, (and not be William F. Buckley, Jr.) you are a rare individual, one in ten thousand.

❀

CORRECT
ANSWERS

abecedarian (ā″bē·sē·dâr′ē·ən)
A. wicket	C. easy	
B. tree-like	D. beastly	(C)

abdominous (ab·dom′ə·nəs)
A. priestly	C. strict	
B. fat	D. dominant	(B)

ablactate (ab·lak′tāt)
A. lubricate	C. scuttle	
B. wean	D. wizen	(B)

abrade (ə·brād′)
A. entwine	C. criticize	
B. condemn	D. rub off	(D)

abstersive (ab·stur′siv)
A. sarcastic	C. sullying	
B. foolish	D. cleansing	(D)

111

accubation (a″kyə·bā′shən, -kyōō-)
    A. assent   C. brooding
    B. reclining   D. hatching   (B)

acerose (as′ə·rōs″)
    A. predominant   C. needle-shaped
    B. foremost   D. serrated   (C)

acescent (ə·ses′ənt)
    A. abating   C. dawning
    B. souring   D. culminating   (B)

aciniform (ə·sin′ə·fôrm″)
    A. clustered   C. flexible
    B. metallic   D. lanky   (A)

actinism (ak′tə·niz″əm)
    A. of sun rays   C. tension
    B. cretinism   D. of blood pressure   (A)

aculeate (ə·kyōō′lē·it, -āt″)
    A. collected   C. displayed
    B. chaff-like   D. sharp-pointed   (D)

adscititious (ad″si·tish′əs)
    A. auspicious   C. superfluous
    B. flavorsome   D. sebaceous   (C)

aduncous (ə·dun′kəs)
    A. tan   C. wet
    B. hooked   D. wailing   (B)

aerie (ār′ē, ēr′ē)
    A. ram-like   C. nest
    B. unshaven   D. spacious   (C)

aesculapian (es″kyə·lā′pē·ən)
    A. medical   C. aesthetic
    B. pornographic   D. effeminate   (A)

afflatus (ə·flā′təs)
    A. expansion   C. insult
    B. boast   D. inspiration   (D)

agravic (ə·grav′ik)
    A. frolicsome   C. flighty
    B. weightless   D. heavy   (B)

112

aleatoric (ā′lē·ə·tōr″ik, -tôr″-)
    A. based upon chance   C. rhetorical
    B. thirst-quenching   D. witty   (A)

algetic (al·jet′ik)
    A. plant-like   C. oily
    B. glossy   D. painful   (D)

algolagnic (al″gə·lag′nik)
    A. bony   C. soothing
    B. greenish   D. masochistic   (D)

allagrugous (a″la·grōō′jəs)
    A. ghastly   C. from within
    B. harmonious   D. natural   (A)

allogenic (al″ə·jen′ik)
    A. hereditary   C. soothing
    B. dissimilar genes   D. causing tearing   (B)

almoner (al′mə·nər, ä′-)
    A. alms-giver   C. peasant
    B. worker   D. beggar   (A)

amaranthine (am″ə·ran′thin, -thīn)
    A. baroque   C. tortuous
    B. immortal   D. oceanic   (B)

amphibolous (am·fib′ə·ləs, am″fə·bol′əs)
    A. murky   C. cold-blooded
    B. tadpole-like   D. equivocal   (D)

ampullaceous (am″pə·lā′shəs)
    A. fowl-like   C. microscopic
    B. globular   D. electrical   B)

amygdaline (ə·mig′də·lin, -līn″)
    A. wrinkled   C. smooth
    B. tortuous   D. almond-like   (D)

anabasis (ə·nab′ə·sis)
    A. treaty   C. trek
    B. retreat   D. advance   (B)

anacreontic (ə·nak″rē·on′tik)
    A. aged   C. jovial
    B. hoary   D. humpbacked   (C)

113

anagogic (an''ə·goj'ik)
    A. mystical   C. musical
    B. illiterate   D. instructive   (A)
analeptic (an''ə·lep'tik)
    A. invigorating   C. ancient
    B. of events   D. fecal   (A)
ananias (an'ə·nī'əs)
    A. liar   C. biblical name
    B. scholar   D. small insect   (A)
anchorite (ang'kə·rīt')
    A. mineral   C. hitching post
    B. hermit   D. arsenal   (B)
ancipital (an·si'pi·təl)
    A. adjoining   C. far away
    B. two-edged   D. parietal   (B)
androgynous (an·droj'ə·nəs)
    A. mythological   C. tedious
    B. oceanic   D. bisexual   (D)
aniconic (an''ī·kon'ik)
    A. seed-eating   C. without idols
    B. primitive   D. amusing   (C)
anile (an'īl, ā'nīl)
    A. chaste   C. faltering
    B. elderly   D. tortuous   (C)
animadversion (an''ə·mad·vur'zhən)
    A. punishment   C. pretext
    B. criticism   D. hatred   (B)
anneal (ə·nēl')
    A. slenderize   C. censure
    B. inflame   D. revoke   (B)
anomy (an'ə·mē'')
    A. senseless   C. of nine
    B. solitary   D. lawlessness   (D)
ansate (an'sāt)
    A. parched   C. copper-like
    B. notched   D. with handle   (D)

anserine (an'sə·rīn″,-rin)
  A. silly
  B. tiresome

C. meat-eating
D. bland   (A)

antelucan (an″tə·lōōk'ən)
  A. after new year
  B. before dawn

C. primitive
D. gnostic   (B)

antephialtic (an″tē·fē·al'tik)
  A. primal
  B. dawning

C. heathen
D. dispelling bad dreams   (D)

antibromic (an″tē·brō'mik)
  A. deodorizing
  B. pungent

C. disquieting
D. curative   (A)

antiphrasis (an·tif'rə·sis)
  A. dissent
  B. iron

C. irony
D. disruption   (C)

antisyzygy (an″ti·siz'i·jē)
  A. grounding
  B. of double value

C. anti-cabalistic
D. union of opposites   (D)

aphesis (af'i·sis)
  A. unfitness
  B. loss of vowels

C. censure
D. laziness   (B)

apocrustic (ap″ə·krust'ik, ap'o-)
  A. astringent
  B. deadly

C. mechanical
D. baiting   (A)

apodictic (ap″ə·dik'tik)
  A. hairless
  B. sour

C. tardy
D. certain   (D)

apolaustic (ap″ə·lôst'ik, ap'o-)
  A. hairy
  B. carking

C. wasteful
D. self-indulgent   (D)

apterous (ap'tər·əs)
  A. innocent
  B. inclined

C. not of land
D. wingless   (D)

aquiline (ak'wə·līn″, -lin)
  A. floating
  B. watery

C. hooked
D. blue   (C)

115

arcadian (är·kā′dē·ən)
    A. simple   C. complex
    B. urbane   D. ruddy   (A)

archly (ärch′lē)
    A. roguish   C. gaily
    B. bow-like   D. haughty   (A)

arcuate (är′kyo͞o·it, -āt″)
    A. metallic   C. seaworthy
    B. curved   D. fiendish   (B)

arenicolous (ar″ə·nik′ə·ləs)
    A. kidney-shaped   C. theatrical
    B. golden   D. inhabiting sand   (D)

argilaceous (är″jə·lā′shəs)
    A. classical   C. clayey
    B. effeminate   D. porous   (C)

argosy (är′gə·sē)
    A. one-eared elephant   C. ancient bird
    B. a ship   D. tale   (B)

argute (är·gyo͞ot′)
    A. shrill   C. occult
    B. tough   D. proper   (A)

astucious (ô·stu′shəs″, -stush′əs)
    A. forgetful   C. bulbous
    B. seated   D. astute   (D)

asyndetic (as′in·det′ik)
    A. without conjunctions C. metric
    B. genuine   D. without rhythm (A)

ataraxic (at″ə·raks′ik)
    A. calm   C. frenetic
    B. strong   D. weak   (A)

attic (at′ik)
    A. elegant   C. hoary
    B. cosmic   D. grave   (A)

augean (ô·jē′ən)
    A. immaculate   C. filthy
    B. heinous   D. rich   (C)

116

auscultation (ô″skəl·tā′shən)
    A. listening   C. sniffing
    B. kissing   D. eating   (A)

austral (ô′strəl)
    A. golden   C. blithe
    B. southern   D. nasal   (B)

autochthonous (ô·tok′thə·nəs)
    A. dictator   C. self-destructive
    B. deadly   D. aboriginal   (D)

autognosis (ô·təg·nō′sis)
    A. self-deception   C. personality
    B. paralysis   D. self-knowledge   (D)

autonomasia (ô″tə·nō·mā′zhə)
    A. independence   C. amnesia
    B. proper name   D. self-respect   (B)

avatar (av″ə·tär′)
    A. celestial motion   C. Greek altar
    B. carnate embodiment   D. salty sailor   (B)

balneal (bal′nē·əl)
    A. hairless   C. of balls
    B. of baths   D. of dancing   (B)

banausic (bə·nô′sik, -zik)
    A. crude   C. utilitarian
    B. queasy   D. distasteful   (C)

bandersnatch (ban′dər·snach″)
    A. joke   C. lampoon
    B. imaginary animal   D. coed   (B)

bastinado (bas″tə·nā′dō)
    A. crib   C. baste
    B. beat with sticks   D. musical instrument   (B)

batten (bat′ən)
    A. steel oneself   C. thrust
    B. filch   D. thrive   (D)

beetling (bēt′ling)
    A. overhanging   C. wretching
    B. small plant   D. machine gun   (A)

117

beldam (bel′dəm)
    A. furor
    C. commotion
    B. old hag
    D. beauty   (B)

belletristic (bel″li·tris′tik)
    A. of Gentile ladies
    C. flighty
    B. war-like
    D. of fine literature   (D)

bezoardic (bē′zōr·dik, -zôr-)
    A. counter-poisonous
    C. tropical
    B. flesh-eating
    D. theatrical   (A)

bibelot (bib′lō)
    A. library
    C. dictionary
    B. artistic object
    D. fop   (B)

bight (bīt)
    A. loop
    C. astigmatism
    B. piece of land
    D. disease   (A)

billingsgate (bil′ingz·gāt″)
    A. vulgar language
    C. pedantic
    B. nightclub
    D. ticket of admission   (A)

blandishment (blan′dish·mənt)
    A. modesty
    C. exploitation
    B. exile
    D. flattery   (D)

bombinate (bom′bə·nāt″)
    A. pompous
    C. contend
    B. deride
    D. buzzing   (D)

borborology (bōr″bōr·ol′ə·jē, bôr′bôr-)
    A. study of pygmies
    C. rumbling sound
    B. glaciation
    D. torpor   (C)

bosky (bos′kē)
    A. haughty
    C. bossy
    B. dusky
    D. having bushes   (D)

brazen (brā′zən)
    A. cross
    C. roast
    B. brass-like
    D. testy   (B)

bromidrosis (brō″mi·drō′sis)
    A. infection
    C. body odor
    B. appeasement
    D. utter despair   (C)

brouhaha (broo·hä′hä, broo″hä·hä′)
A. disease	C. potion
B. noisy uproar	D. a chant (B)

brumal (broo′məl)
A. of brooms	C. wintry
B. elegant	D. basic (C)

brummagem (brum′ə·jəm)
A. bounty	C. showy
B. tailored	D. rare stone (C)

buccal (buk′əl)
A. agrarian	C. cavernous
B. pastoral	D. of the cheek (D)

buncombe (bung′kəm)
A. lady's man	C. facile
B. empty speech	D. propaganda (B)

burlesque (bər·lesk′)
A. disrobing	C. coating
B. mocking	D. questioning (B)

bursiform (bur′sə·fôrm″)
A. brassiere	C. money-grubbing
B. supporting	D. pouch-like (D)

bushido (boo′she·dô′)
A. fecal	C. woodsy
B. Samurai code	D. culinary (B)

bustluscious (bust·lush′əs)
A. resonant	C. broke
B. ripen	D. stacked (D)

cachinnation (kak″in·nā′shən)
A. discord	C. implosion
B. function	D. laughter (D)

cadge (kaj)
A. beaver-like	C. coquet
B. peddle	D. insignia (B)

caducous (kə·doo′kəs, -dyoo′-)
A. circular	C. medicinal
B. deciduous	D. glittering (B)

119

cairn (kārn)
    A. mound of stones   C. hermit
    B. knowledge   D. nurse   (A)
caitiff (kā′tif)
    A. emir   C. servile
    B. wicked   D. whimsical   (B)
calescent (kə·les′ənt)
    A. warming   C. dietary
    B. glowing   D. western   (A)
caliginous (kə·lij′ə·nəs)
    A. throaty   C. vaginal
    B. misty   D. bursting   (B)
calligraphy (kə·lig′rə·fē)
    A. penmanship   C. radiograph
    B. semantics   D. telegraphy   (A)
callipygous (kəl″ə·pī′gəs)
    A. Romanesque   C. shapely rump
    B. feathered   D. open-ended   (C)
calumet (kal′yə·met″, kal″yə·met′)
    A. meeting hall   C. scale
    B. weight   D. peace pipe   (D)
camarilla (kam″ə·ril′ə)
    A. baby dromedary   C. frilly
    B. yellow-green   D. clique   (D)
campanulate (kam·pan′yə·lit, -lāt″)
    A. spatulate   C. countrified
    B. bell-shaped   D. brotherly   (B)
candent (kan′dənt)
    A. blowsy   C. stained
    B. glowing   D. yellowish   (B)
canny (kan′ē)
    A. buxom   C. witty
    B. sarcastic   D. shrewd   (D)
caparison (kə·par′i·sən)
    A. dual   C. assail
    B. adorn   D. finish   (B)

caprylic (kə·pril'ik, ka-)
    A. sunny   C. oval
    B. animal odor   D. Italian   **(B)**

captious (kap'shəs)
    A. tricky   C. resolute
    B. rebellious   D. surly   **(A)**

carbecue (kär'bə·kyoo'')
    A. rifle range   C. auto parts
    B. salvaging device   D. car wash   **(B)**

carious (kār'ē·əs)
    A. decayed   C. vexing
    B. wary   D. careful   **(A)**

carking (kär'king)
    A. railing   C. shouting
    B. complaining   D. perplexing   **(D)**

carillon (kar'ə·lon'', -lən)
    A. garment   C. color
    B. fixed bells   D. child's lullabye   **(B)**

carousal (kə·rou'zəl)
    A. mull over   C. glance over
    B. boat trip   D. drinking party   **(D)**

caryatid (kar''ē·at'id)
    A. gem   C. column
    B. ladybug   D. lattice   **(C)**

caterwaul (kat'ər·wôl'')
    A. skipping gingerly   C. wailing
    B. complaining   D. regulating   **(C)**

cathexis (kə·thek'sis)
    A. nub   C. nexus
    B. emotional investment D. cathode   **(B)**

caudate (kô'dāt)
    A. tailless   C. bald
    B. furry   D. having a tail   **(D)**

caudle (kôd'əl)
    A. curl   C. warm drink
    B. cozen   D. coddle   **(C)**

121

causerie (kō''zə·rē', kô''-)
    A. chat   C. cause
    B. apology   D. dispute   **(A)**

ceraceous (sə·rā'shəs)
    A. oriental   C. waxy
    B. shiny   D. biracial   **(C)**

cerebration (ser''ə·brā'shən)
    A. shiver   C. quake
    B. thought   D. soiree   **(B)**

cernuous (surn'yōō·əs, sur'nōō-)
    A. drooping   C. cautious
    B. shrewd   D. hesitant   **(A)**

charnel (chär'nəl)
    A. silo   C. animal den
    B. burnt umber   D. burial place   **(D)**

chiastic (kī·as'tik)
    A. tubular   C. old-fashioned
    B. mystical   D. reversed word order   **(D)**

chiromancy (kī·rə·man''sē)
    A. love of fire   C. idol worship
    B. palmistry   D. sleight of hand   **(B)**

chthonic (thon'ik)
    A. atomic   C. ghostly
    B. sluggish   D. droopy   **(C)**

cimmerian (si·mēr'ē·ən)
    A. volatile   C. aboriginal
    B. gloomy   D. caustic   **(B)**

cinerary (sin'ə·rer''ē)
    A. of ashes   C. of movies
    B. mournfully   D. spiced   **(A)**

circadian (sur''kə·dē'ən)
    A. biological cycle   C. of circles
    B. righteous   D. of longitude   **(A)**

cleave (klēv)
    A. crack   C. separate
    B. cling   D. bend   **(B)**

clubbable (klub'ə·bəl)
    A. made of wood   C. clandestine
    B. vociferous   D. sociable   (D)
coeval (kō·ē'vəl)
    A. ancient   C. farm insect
    B. contemporaneous   D. partner   (B)
comatulid (kə·mach'ə·lid)
    A. curled hair   C. comatose
    B. sleepy   D. neat   (A)
comitology (kə''mit·ol'ə·jē)
    A. astrology   C. concerning sleep
    B. study of committees   D. branch of astronomy   (B)
comminatory (kə·min'ə·tōr''ē, -tôr''-)
    A. denunciatory   C. homely
    B. complimentary   D. praiseworthy   (A)
concatenate (kon·kat'ə·nāt'')
    A. connected   C. buoyant
    B. spotted   D. sprawling   (A)
concinnity (kən·sin'i·tē)
    A. metallic   C. confluence
    B. internal harmony   D. preponderance   (B)
confabulate (kən·fab'yə·lāt'')
    A. chat   C. exaggerate
    B. fib   D. prevaricate   (A)
consuetude (kon'swi·tōōd''-tyōōd'')
    A. constriction   C. shyness
    B. custom   D. demeanor   (B)
contemn (kən·tem')
    A. impugn   C. despise
    B. belie   D. encompass   (C)
conurbation (kən''ur·bā'shən)
    A. swelling   C. tree
    B. urban area   D. hospital zone   (B)
convallariaceous (kən''və·lār''ē·ā'shəs)
    A. of lilies   C. renitent
    B. cross   D. excellent   (A)

123

coprophilia (ko″pro·fil′ē·ə, -fēl′yə)
    A. interest in feces   C. cupric
    B. love of pots   D. love of Copts   (A)

cornigerous (kōr·ni′jər·əs, kôr-)
    A. tree-like   C. having horns
    B. seedless   D. of corns   (C)

cosmopolite (koz·mop′ə·līt″)
    A. alien   C. planet
    B. star   D. citizen of the world   (D)

costive (kos′tiv, kô′stiv)
    A. abrasive   C. constipated
    B. greedy   D. exorbitant   (C)

cozen (kuz′ən)
    A. cheat   C. sidle
    B. defile   D. relative   (A)

crabbed (krab′id, krabd)
    A. aching   C. mislead
    B. stunned   D. peevish   (D)

crapulous (krap′yoo·ləs, -yə-)
    A. shoddy   C. of craps
    B. debauched   D. miserable   (B)

creatic (krē·at′ik)
    A. of flesh   C. sublime
    B. inventive   D. original   (A)

crepitate (krep′i·tāt″)
    A. sunset   C. wizened
    B. hoary   D. crackle   (D)

crepuscular (kri·pus′kyə·lər)
    A. of blood   C. fluid
    B. miniscule   D. of twilight   (D)

croesus (krē′səs)
    A. wealthy man   C. soldier
    B. secretary   D. hobo   (A)

cryotherapy (krī″ō·ther′ə·pē)
    A. bather   C. treat with cold
    B. massage   D. treat with heat   (C)

124

cudgel (kuj'əl)
    A. animal cub   C. heavy club
    B. opera glass   D. spoon'   (C)

cunctation (kungk·tā'shən)
    A. delay   C. tremor
    B. distortion   D. panting   (A)

cuneal (kyōō'nē·əl)
    A. of script   C. of space
    B. of scabs   D. wedge-like   (D)

cupreous (kyōō'prē·əs, kōō'-)
    A. hollow   C. loveable
    B. copper-like   D. brittle   (B)

curioso (kyoor"ē·ō'sō)
    A. amateur   C. necklace
    B. summary   D. expert   (A)

curmudgeon (kər·muj'ən)
    A. sore   C. club
    B. little bit   D. surly fellow   (D)

cursive (kur'siv)
    A. flowing script   C. epithetical
    B. summary   D. temporary   (A)

cynophobia (sī'nə·fō"bē·ə)
    A. fear of dogs   C. fear of bears
    B. fear of cats   D. fear of cliffs   (A)

cynosure (sī'nə·shoor", sin'ə-)
    A. easy job   C. favoritism
    B. center of interest   D. constellation   (B)

declivous (di·klī'vəs)
    A. musical   C. scrawny
    B. sloping down   D. grasping   (B)

decoct (di·kokt')
    A. fabricate   C. hide from
    B. dissimulate   D. extract the essence   (D)

decrement (dek'rə·mənt)
    A. cease   C. declare
    B. decrease   D. ten years   (B)

125

decussate (di·kus′āt)
    A. trim
    B. prune

    C. crossed
    D. undressed   (C)

defenestration (dē·fen″i·strā′shən)
    A. abolish
    B. surrender

    C. defense
    D. eject from a window   (D)

deglutition (dē″gloo·tish′ən)
    A. swallowing
    B. sneezing

    C. bloodletting
    D. overeating   (A)

delator (di·lā′tər)
    A. informer
    B. assistant

    C. actor
    D. medical instrument   (A)

deliquesce (del′ə·kwəs)
    A. dry up
    B. freeze

    C. melt
    D. harden   (C)

delitescent (del″i·tes′ənt)
    A. spurious
    B. inactive

    C. obscure
    D. not kosher   (B)

deltiologist (del″tē·ol′ə·jist)
    A. fraternity man
    B. scientist

    C. farmer
    D. collector of postcards   (D)

deracinate (di·ras′ə·nat″)
    A. uproot
    B. fertilize

    C. reveal
    D. chide   (A)

dilate (dī·lāt′, di-)
    A. delay
    B. open

    C. startle
    D. expatiate   (D)

dimidiate (di·mid′ē·āt″, dī-, -it)
    A. cut in half
    B. apologize

    C. intervene
    D. abate   (A)

dimissory (dim′i·sor″ē, -sôr′-)
    A. evasive
    B. remiss

    C. dismissing
    D. ineffective   (C)

discalced (dis·kalst′)
    A. discounted
    B. barefoot

    C. subtracted
    D. shaved   (B)

discommode (dis"kə·mōd')
 A. evict   C. strip
 B. annoy   D. villify   (B)
disquisition (dis"kwi·zish'ən)
 A. essay   C. lecture
 B. formal inquiry   D. apology   (B)
distaff (dis'taf, -täf)
 A. surly   C. complex
 B. women's work   D. dethrone   (B)
diva (dē'vä)
 A. guru   C. tenderfoot
 B. prima donna   D. scholar   (B)
divagate (dī'və·gāt")
 A. wander   C. infer
 B. dig   D. operate   (A)
doggerel (dô'gər·əl, dog'ər-)
 A. cavil   C. complaint
 B. grunt   D. irregular poetry   (D)
dollop (dol'əp)
 A. lump   C. smack
 B. fowl   D. lash   (A)
dontopedalogy (don·tə·ped·al'ə·jē)
 A. foolish statements   C. bone disease
 B. dinosaur   D. cattle affliction   (A)
draconian (drā·kō'nē·ən)
 A. cruel   C. pompous
 B. lengthy   D. winding   (A)
draconic (drā·kon'ik)
 A. of stars   C. dragon-like
 B. colorful   D. mountainous   (C)
drogue (drōg)
 A. oil   C. blubber
 B. sea anchor   D. accent   (B)
dromomania (drō·mə·mā'nē·ə, -mān'yə)
 A. longing for travel   C. love of bees
 B. of camels   D. love of cake   (A)

127

dudgeon (duj'ən)
    A. prison   C. resentment
    B. ember   D. flail   (C)

dumpish (dum'pish)
    A. ruinous   C. fat
    B. stupid   D. skinny   (B)

dystopia (dis·tō'·pē·ə)
    A. ear disease   C. insipid
    B. blindness   D. miserable place   (D)

ecdysiast (ek·diz'ē·ast")
    A. gym teacher   C. animal
    B. stripper   D. fisherman   (B)

echinate (ek'ə·nāt", -nit)
    A. spiny   C. smooth
    B. paste   D. old   (A)

edentate (ē·den'tāt)
    A. salty   C. tropical
    B. divine   D. toothless   (D)

empyreal (em·pir'ē·əl, em'pə·rē-)
    A. Roman   C. powerful
    B. heavenly   D. conquering   (B)

encincture (en·singk'chər)
    A. destroy   C. encircle
    B. overcome   D. conclude   (C)

energumen (en"ər·gyoo'mən)
    A. one possessed   C. dynamo
    B. ore   D. poetic meter   (A)

epexegetic (ep·ek"si·jet'ik)
    A. conclusive   C. conducive
    B. explanatory   D. rhythmic   (B)

ephebic (i·fē'bik, e-)
    A. flowery   C. adolescent
    B. cholic   D. allergic   (C)

epicene (ep'i·sēn")
    A. extinct   C. tropical
    B. hermaphrodite   D. bushy   (B)

epidictic (ep″i·dik′tik)
  A. convulsive
  B. following

  C. recent
  D. displaying the skill of   (D)

epithalamium (ep″ə·thə·lā′mē·əm)
  A. surface coat
  B. organ

  C. ode
  D. marital song   (D)

epizeuxis (ep″i·zo͞ok′səs)
  A. terror
  B. aftermath

  C. emphatic repetition
  D. geological age   (C)

eponym (ep′ə·nim)
  A. era
  B. part of speech

  C. horse-like
  D. original name   (D)

erectarine (i·rek′tə·rēn″)
  A. pogo stick
  B. fruit

  C. game
  D. rhythm instrument   (D)

eristic (e·ris′tik)
  A. upper class
  B. controversial

  C. of relaxation
  D. bland   (B)

erose (i·rōs′)
  A. uneven
  B. comical

  C. risk
  D. cherubic   (A)

eructation (i·ruk·tā′shən, ē′-)
  A. interjection
  B. coarseness

  C. blemish
  D. belching   (D)

esculent (es′kyə·lənt)
  A. effete
  B. edible

  C. nonpotable
  D. perceptive   (B)

estivate (es′tə·vāt″)
  A. graze
  B. stimulate

  C. assess
  D. pass the summer   (D)

esurient (i·soor′ē·ənt)
  A. sentient
  B. hungry

  C. luxurious
  D. wintry   (B)

euphuistic (yo͞o′fyo͞o·is′tik)
  A. banal
  B. understatement

  C. tributory
  D. affected speech   (D)

129

excrementitious (ek"skrə·mən·tish'əs)
- A. fecal
- B. evasive
- C. integral
- D. outside   (A)

excrescent (ik·skres'ənt)
- A. superfluous
- B. erase
- C. ordinary
- D. strike out   (A)

exigible (ek'si·jə·bəl)
- A. claimable
- B. alive
- C. superfluous
- D. dependent   (A)

exoteric (ek"sə·ter'ik)
- A. outlandish
- B. complex
- C. peripheral
- D. easily understood   (D)

facinorous (fə·sin'ər·əs)
- A. wicked
- B. easy
- C. noble
- D. scheming   (A)

factotum (fak·tō'təm)
- A. trifle
- B. handyman
- C. handbag
- D. graven image   (B)

falcate (fal'kāt)
- A. patronize
- B. default
- C. crescent-shaped
- D. depreciate   (C)

fanfaronade (fan"fə·rə·nād')
- A. Philistine
- B. bluster
- C. fancy
- D. grandeur   (B)

farctate (färk'tāt)
- A. stuffed full
- B. reform
- C. bloat
- D. impede   (A)

farrago (fə·rä'gō, -rā'-)
- A. expert
- B. hodgepodge
- C. shrew
- D. interloper   (B)

fatidic (fā·tid'ik, fə-)
- A. logical
- B. easy
- C. efficient
- D. prophetic   (D)

feracious (fə·rā'shəs)
- A. debauched
- B. brutal
- C. ruthless
- D. fruitful   (D)

130

fescennine (fes'ə·nīn″, -nin)

    A. obscene

    B. viscious

    C. maudlin

    D. ironic   **(A)**

festoon (fe·stoon′)

    A. dispute

    B. pierce

    C. decorate with flowers

    D. joke   **(C)**

filipendulous (fil″ə·pen′jə·ləs, -də·ləs)

    A. estimable

    B. hanging

    C. meretricious

    D. incomplete   **(B)**

flagitious (flə·jish′əs)

    A. magical

    B. heinous

    C. brave

    D. commonplace   **(B)**

floccilation (flok″sə·lā′shən)

    A. delirious picking

    B. mercy

    C. lessening

    D. billowing   **(A)**

floccinaucinihilipilification (good luck)

    A. disease

    B. of hair

    C. self-hatred

    D. estimating nil   **(D)**

flummox (flum′əks)

    A. gargle

    B. yak

    C. mix

    D. abash   **(D)**

forficate (fôr′fə·kit, -kāt″)

    A. blacken

    B. forked

    C. harden

    D. surrender   **(B)**

fribble (frib′əl)

    A. squander

    B. drool

    C. paltry

    D. haggle   **(C)**

frigorific (frig″ə·rif′ik)

    A. frightful

    B. offensive

    C. causing cold

    D. marvelous   **(C)**

froward (frō′wərd, -ərd)

    A. beldam

    B. frantic

    C. suspicious

    D. perverse   **(D)**

frowzy (frou′zē)

    A. slovenly

    B. drunken

    C. lazy

    D. contemptuous   **(A)**

131

fructuous (fruk′choo·əs)
 A. docile   C. sweet
 B. profitable   D. resilient   (B)

frugivorous (frōō·jiv′ər·əs)
 A. wild   C. productive
 B. fruit-eating   D. frugal   (B)

fugacious (fyōō·gā′shəs)
 A. abrupt   C. enduring
 B. ephemeral   D. ferocious   (B)

fulgurous (ful′gyər·əs)
 A. rebellious   C. lightning-like
 B. credible   D. stout   (C)

fumacious (fyōō·mā′shəs)
 A. noisome   C. nasty
 B. fond of smoking D. gaseous   (B)

funambulist (fyōō·nam′byə·list)
 A. juggler   C. magician
 B. clown   D. tightrope walker (D)

funicular (fyōō·nik′yə·lər)
 A. spiral   C. geography
 B. ascending   D. of a cord   (D)

furfuraceous (fur″fyoo·rā′shəs)
 A. obedient   C. wooly
 B. scaly   D. prolonged   (B)

gallimaufry (gal″ə·mô′frē)
 A. mistake   C. correction
 B. piddle   D. jumble   (D)

gallinaceous (gal″ə·nā′shəs)
 A. naked   C. yellow
 B. fowl-like   D. Irish   (B)

galumph (gə·lumf′)
 A. move clumsily   C. sigh
 B. gallop   D. hyphenate   (A)

galumptious (gə·lump′shəs)
 A. tasty   C. first-rate
 B. huge   D. despicable (C)

gasconade (gas″kə·nād′)
    A. of Italy   C. tender
    B. bluster   D. outrage   **(B)**

gawkocracy (gôk·ok′rə·sē)
    A. mob rule   C. of disbelief
    B. state of fear   D. T.V. viewers   **(D)**

gewgaw (gyōō′gô, gōō′-)
    A. showy   C. modern
    B. spoken   D. health   **(A)**

gibbous (gib′əs, jib′-)
    A. humpbacked   C. horned
    B. abstract   D. lakeside   **(A)**

girning (gur′ning)
    A. smiling   C. snarling
    B. coughing   D. escaping   **(C)**

glabrous (glā′brəs)
    A. grassy   C. showy
    B. bald   D. evil   **(B)**

glitch (glich)
    A. wound   C. hickey
    B. malfunction   D. abrasion   **(B)**

glutinous (glōōt′ə·nəs)
    A. sticky   C. rabid
    B. excessive   D. labile   **(A)**

glyptic (glip′tik)
    A. abbreviated   C. historical
    B. crude   D. engraving   **(D)**

gnathic (nath′ik)
    A. harsh   C. of the jaw
    B. sharp   D. racial   **(C)**

gnathonic (na·thon′ik)
    A. valorous   C. harmonious
    B. fawning   D. roundabout   **(B)**

gnomic (nō′mik, nom′ik)
    A. pithy   C. evil
    B. lively   D. circular   **(A)**

gobbledygook (gob″əl·dē·gook′)

    A. stilted talk   C. turkey

    B. mess   D. mixture   (A)

gongoozler (gon·gōōz′lər)

    A. one who stares   C. rascal

    B. chicken thief   D. smuggler   (A)

gorgon (gor′gən)

    A. knotty problem   C. ugly woman

    B. employer   D. beast   (C)

gratulant (grach′ə·lənt)

    A. humble   C. expressing joy

    B. sated   D. jewelled   (C)

graveolent (grə·vē′əl·ənt)

    A. evasive   C. beleaguered

    B. fetid   D. truculent   (B)

gravid (grav′id)

    A. extreme   C. wasteful

    B. deepening   D. pregnant   (D)

gravific (gra·vif′ik)

    A. worsening   C. makes heavy

    B. augury   D. serious   (C)

gregarian (gri·gār′ē·ən)

    A. by hand   C. hortatory

    B. common   D. talkative   (B)

gressorial (gre·sōr′ē·əl, -sôr′-)

    A. reclining   C. plundering

    B. aggressive   D. ambulatory   (D)

gynecoid (gī′nə·koid″, jin′ə-)

    A. athletic   C. shapely

    B. womanish   D. childlike   (B)

hagiophobia (hag″ē·ō·fō′bē·ə)

    A. fear of holy things   C. fear of hospitals

    B. fear of maps   D. fear of black magic   (A)

hallucal (hal′yə·kəl)

    A. famous   C. resonant

    B. of the big toe   D. of ampitheatres   (B)

134

hardihood (här'dē·hood″)
   A. affable   C. stability
   B. boldness   D. passionate   (B)

hebdomadal (heb·dom'ə·dəl)
   A. Arabic   C. monthly
   B. Jewish   D. weekly   (D)

hebetic (hi·bet'ik)
   A. irritable   C. of puberty
   B. of herbs   D. soothing agent   (C)

hebetude (heb'i·tood″, -tyood″)
   A. silence   C. Semitism
   B. insolence   D. lethargy   (D)

hecatomb (hek'ə·tōm″, -toom″)
   A. thousand   C. ruins
   B. a grave   D. slaughter   (D)

helicoid (hel'ə·koid″, hē'lə-)
   A. weightless   C. spiral
   B. Greek coin   D. rhomboid   (C)

hesperian (he·spēr'ē·ən)
   A. western   C. seaworthy
   B. southern   D. wind-blown   (A)

heuristic (hyoo·ris'tik)
   A. timely   C. instructive
   B. orderly   D. medicinal   (C)

hiemal (hī'ə·məl)
   A. grizzled   C. wintry
   B. hoary   D. female membrane   (C)

hieratic (hī″ə·rat'ik, hī·rat'-)
   A. priestly   C. limitless
   B. servile   D. orderly   (A)

hobbledehoy (hob'əl·dē·hoi″)
   A. tottering   C. broken down
   B. stripling   D. lame   (B)

hogmanay (hog″mə·nā')
   A. rural   C. New Year's Eve
   B. fodder   D. fertilizer   (C)

135

hoity-toity (hoi′tē·toi′tē)
    A. uppity   C. musical instrument
    B. giddy   D. pesky   (B)
hokeypokey (hō′kē·pō′kē)
    A. pigsty   C. nonsense
    B. lethargy   D. deception   (D)
horripilation (hô·rip″ə·lā′shən, ho-)
    A. ghastly   C. gooseflesh
    B. fearful   D. wavelength   (C)
horrisonous (hô·ris′ən·əs)
    A. fearful   C. bombastic
    B. discordant   D. far off   (B)
hortulan (ho′chə·lən)
    A. of a garden   C. tactless
    B. snotty   D. advisory   (A)
hubristic (hyoo·bris′tik, hoo′bris-)
    A. wild   C. urban
    B. central   D. insolent   (D)
hypnagogic (hip″nə·goj′ik)
    A. expansive   C. inducing sleep
    B. haphazard   D. immense   (C)
hypnopompic (hip″nə·pom′pik)
    A. waking   C. grandiose
    B. central   D. contradictory (A)
ignicolist (ig·ni·kō′list)
    A. hard stone   C. miser
    B. firefly   D. fire-worshipper (D)
illative (il′ə·tiv, i·lā′-)
    A. possible   C. practical
    B. inferential   D. native   (B)
imbrication (im″brə·kā′shən)
    A. stealth   C. an overlapping
    B. contempt   D. civilization   (C)
imbrue (im·broo′)
    A. strive   C. accrue
    B. stain   D. lock in   (B)

immanent (im′ə·nənt)
    A. momentary
    B. secure

C. fresh
D. inherent   **(D)**

immund (ə·mənd′)
    A. dull
    B. reject

C. expunge
D. unclean   **(D)**

impavid (im·pav′id)
    A. wealthy
    B. fearless

C. proud
D. stern   **(B)**

inanition (in″ə·nish′ən)
    A. hope
    B. defile

C. being empty
D. valueless   **(C)**

incrassate (in·kras′āt)
    A. thicken
    B. loot

C. shock
D. illiterate   **(A)**

indehiscent (in″di·his′ənt)
    A. not opening
    B. restricted

C. unexplained
D. not kosher   **(A)**

inexpugnable (in″ik·spug′nə·bəl)
    A. impossible
    B. haughty

C. voluble
D. unconquerable   **(D)**

infralapsarianism (good luck)
    A. religious doctrine
    B. scientific law

C. illness
D. kingly rule   **(A)**

infundibular (in″fun·dib′yə·lər)
    A. pillaged
    B. endless

C. funnel-shaped
D. precise   **(C)**

ingeminate (in·jem′ə·nāt″)
    A. reiterate
    B. unequal

C. passive
D. impose   **(A)**

intellection (in″tə·lek′shən)
    A. knowledge
    B. cavalcade

C. question
D. thinking   **(D)**

intumescence (in″tōō·mes′əns, -tyoo-)
    A. oppression
    B. swelling up

C. glowing
D. stubbornness   **(B)**

137

ioblepharous (ī·ə·ble′fär·əs)
    A. merciful   C. violet-lidded
    B. pompous   D. colonial   (C)

irenic (ī·ren′ik, -rē′nik)
    A. moral   C. enigmatic
    B. peaceful   D. down-to-earth   (B)

irrefragable (i·ref′rə·gə·bəl)
    A. confidential   C. uncertain
    B. speculative   D. undeniable   (D)

irrefrangible (ir″i·fran′jə·bəl)
    A. deviating   C. emotional
    B. inviolable   D. unbreakable   (B)

isagogic (ī″sə·goj′ik)
    A. theoretical   C. formidable
    B. conscious   D. introductory   (D)

jactation (jak·tā′shən)
    A. boasting   C. splendor
    B. terror   D. prosperity   (A)

janissaries (jan′i·ser″ēz)
    A. explorers   C. prisoners
    B. soldiers   D. thieves   (B)

jape (jāp)
    A. blanch   C. garrison
    B. stare   D. jest   (D)

jehu (jē′hyōō)
    A. railway   C. reckless driver
    B. outpost   D. sweet pastry   (C)

jejune (ji·jōōn′)
    A. insipid   C. massive
    B. slender   D. obvious   (A)

jeremiad (jer″ə·mī′ad)
    A. usher   C. palatial
    B. lament   D. monarch   (B)

jerkwater (jurk′wô″tər, -wot″ər)
    A. unbosom   C. insignificant
    B. discharge   D. thunderstruck   (C)

138

jugal (jōō′gəl)
    A. marital
    B. toothy

C. harmonious
D. of the cheek   (D)

jugulate (jōō′gyə·lāt″)
    A. spring
    B. suppress

C. construct
D. excite   (B)

katabasis (kə·tab′ə·sis)
    A. retreat
    B. await

C. despoil
D. exhibition   (A)

labefaction (lab″ə·fak′shən)
    A. fame
    B. ransom

C. glee
D. weakening   (D)

labile (lā′bil)
    A. smooth
    B. facile

C. unstable
D. doubtful   (C)

lacustrine (lə·kus′trin)
    A. winding
    B. felicitous

C. apt
D. of lakes   (D)

lagniappe (lan·yap′, lan′yap)
    A. rare meat
    B. gratuitous gift

C. salve
D. urchin   (B)

lallation (la·lā′shən)
    A. growl
    B. torpor

C. slavery
D. speech impediment   (D)

lanate (lā′nāt)
    A. wooly
    B. fallen

C. lonely
D. golden   (A)

lanuginous (lə·nōōj′ə·nəs, -nyōō′-)
    A. proud
    B. covered with down

C. loose gravy
D. jagged   (B)

laodicean (lā·od″i·sē′ən, lā″ə·di·sē′ən)
    A. indifferent
    B. bashful

C. deep sea
D. zestful   (A)

latitudinarian (lat″i·tōōd″ə·nâr′ē·ən, -tyōōd″-)
    A. old man
    B. liberal

C. wide area
D. courtier   (B)

lenticular (len·tik′yə·lər)
    A. of a lens
    C. fasting season
    B. portly
    D. bashful
    (A)

lentiginous (len·ti j′ə·nəs)
    A. almond-shaped
    C. freckled
    B. slender
    D. peaceful
    (C)

leptodactylous (lep″tə·dak′til·əs)
    A. having slender toes
    C. spotted
    B. fish-eating
    D. crippled
    (A)

lethiferous (li·thif′ər·əs)
    A. pensive
    C. bland
    B. deadly
    D. cloaking
    (B)

lilting (lilt′ing)
    A. lively
    C. figurative
    B. wilting
    D. leaning
    (A)

limn (lim)
    A. mistake
    C. brazen
    B. morbid
    D. portray
    (D)

litotes (lī′tə·tēz″, -tō-, lit′ə-)
    A. singular
    C. baubles
    B. understatement
    D. bodyguards
    (B)

logodaedaly (lô″gə·dē′də·lē)
    A. amusement
    C. verbose
    B. cunning speech
    D. silent
    (B)

lotic (lō′tik)
    A. following
    C. discordant
    B. morbid
    D. living in fast currents
    (D)

lucubration (lōō″kyoo·brā′shən)
    A. torpor
    C. laborious work
    B. foul speech
    D. child's play
    (C)

luculent (lōō′kyoo·lənt)
    A. obscure
    C. muddy
    B. clear
    D. downstream
    (B)

macaronic (mak″ə·ron′ik)
    A. jumbled
    C. infantile
    B. abrasive
    D. grovelling
    (A)

140

macrotous (mak·rot′əs)
    A. filthy   C. plastic
    B. gigantic   D. large-eared   (D)

mactation (mak·tā′shən)
    A. sacrificing   C. inherent
    B. idle   D. absorbing   (A)

maculate (mak′yə·lit)
    A. clean   C. spotted
    B. feast   D. dried   (C)

maieutic (mā·yoo′tik)
    A. urban   C. deadly
    B. evoking ideas   D. blind   (B)

malic (mal′ik, mā′lik)
    A. of apples   C. of bad temper
    B. courteous   D. curious   (A)

mammon (mam′ən)
    A. reward   C. lustful
    B. wealth   D. flat   (B)

mansuetude (man′swi·tood″, -tyood″)
    A. devotion   C. freedom
    B. pride   D. gentleness   (D)

mantic (man′tik)
    A. of divination   C. seaworthy
    B. mainland   D. unchallenged   (A)

marasmic (mə·raz′mik)
    A. cooking   C. wasting
    B. newsy   D. relentless   (C)

marcescent (mär·ses′ənt)
    A. liquid   C. salty
    B. turning green   D. withering   (D)

marigenous (mə·rij′ə·nəs)
    A. of the sea   C. lofty
    B. consuming green cheese   D. slippery   (A)

marmoreal (mär·mōr′ē·əl, -môr′-)
    A. logical   C. of marble
    B. heavy   D. ostensible   (C)

141

marplot (mär′plot″)
    A. meddler   C. chasten
    B. tomb   D. cabal   (A)

matutinal (mə′tōōt′ə·nəl, -tyōōt′-)
    A. bitter   C. instructive
    B. maternal   D. early   (D)

mawkish (mô′kish)
    A. frenetic   C. sneering
    B. base   D. sentimental   (D)

melic (mel′ik)
    A. lyric   C. gentle
    B. fluent   D. of apples   (A)

melliferous (mə·lif′ər·əs)
    A. fluent   C. smooth of gait
    B. yielding honey   D. verbose   (B)

mendicity (men·dis′i·tē)
    A. begging   C. lying
    B. candor   D. pride   (A)

mephitic (mə·fit′ik)
    A. oily   C. evil
    B. musty   D. noxious   (D)

minatory (min′ə·tōr″ē, -tôr″-)
    A. important   C. delaying
    B. threatening   D. strike   (B)

moil (moil)
    A. embroil   C. fertile
    B. drudgery   D. assistant   (B)

moloch (mō′lək)
    A. primitive   C. sea shell
    B. demanding system   D. of Hinduism (B)

moondoggle (mōōn′dog″əl)
    A. plot   C. a bird
    B. a dance   D. useless exploration (D)

morbific (môr·bif′ik)
    A. pale   C. causing sickness
    B. superior   D. disgusting   (C)

mordant (môr'dənt)
    A. intense   C. caustic
    B. frightful   D. morbid   (C)
morganatic (môr"gə·nat'ik)
    A. swollen   C. of pirates
    B. huge   D. mixed marriage   (D)
mugwump (mug'wump")
    A. an independent   C. militant
    B. passivist   D. conservative   (A)
mulct (mulkt)
    A. drain   C. weaken
    B. to fine   D. bleed   (B)
muliebrity (myoo"lē·eb'ri·tē)
    A. stubbornness   C. joviality
    B. drunkenness   D. womanhood   (D)
napiform (nā'pə·fôrm")
    A. spiral   C. curly
    B. wispy   D. turnip-shaped   (D)
narial (nār'ē·əl)
    A. of the nostrils   C. vacant
    B. bleak   D. of snails   (A)
nates (nā'tez)
    A. tendrils   C. nostrils
    B. ear lobes   D. buttocks   (D)
neanthropic (nē"ən·throp'ik)
    A. ancient   C. clammy
    B. torpid   D. human   (D)
nescience (nesh'ē·əns)
    A. religion   C. magic
    B. ignorance   D. theory   (B)
nettle (net'əl)
    A. vex   C. a gear
    B. a grain   D. mollify   (A)
nictitate (nik'ti·tāt")
    A. clot   C. wink
    B. prepare   D. falsify   (C)

143

CORRECT
ANSWERS

nidificate (nid'ə·fə·kāt'')
 A. make a nest   C. conceal
 B. fly   D. totally erase (A)
niggling (nig'ling)
 A. carping   C. offensive
 B. petty   D. bargaining (B)
nimiety (ni·mī'i·tē)
 A. pallor   C. excess
 B. timidity   D. dearth (C)
nodus (nō'dəs)
 A. bus stop   C. vacation
 B. wart   D. knotty problem (D)
noetic (nō·et'ik)
 A noble   C. of the mind
 B. gay   D. extremely lazy (C)
nostomania (nos''tə·mā'nē·ə, -mān'yə)
 A. lively   C. boredom
 B. homesickness   D. craving for nuts (B)
novate (nō'vāt)
 A. decline   C. annex
 B. marry   D. replace (D)
novercal (nō·vur'kəl)
 A. hymn   C. of thrones
 B. new   D. stepmotherly (D)
nuchal (nook'əl, nyoo'-)
 A. nape of the neck C. none
 B. beyond   D. void (A)
nulliparous (nu·lip'ər·əs)
 A. ambitious   C. dull
 B. childless   D. perilous (B)
nutant (noot'ənt, nyoot''-)
 A. fraternal   C. flowing
 B. drooping   D. crawling (B)
nympholepsy (nim'fə·lep''sē)
 A. loneliness   C. despair
 B. agony   D. hopeless desire (D)

obbligato (ob''lə·gä′tō, ôb''blē·gä′tô)
    A. servile   C. leap of faith
    B. accompaniment   D. deep bow   (B)

obconic (ob·kon′ik)
    A. pear-shaped   C. ribald
    B. circular   D. queer   (A)

obsecrate (ob′sə·krāt'')
    A. abhor   C. destroy
    B. beseech   D. decay   (B)

obsequy (ob′sə·kwē)
    A. funeral rite   C. scandal
    B. secret   D. confluence   (A)

obstruent (ob′strōō·ənt)
    A. perverse   C. hindering
    B. wierd   D. lazy   (C)

obtund (ob·tund′)
    A. surround   C. relieve
    B. blunt   D. bewilder   (B)

ocellate (os′ə·lāt'', ō·sel′it)
    A. spiny   C. bony
    B. spotted   D. having claws (B)

ochlocracy (ok·lok′rə·sē)
    A. dictatorship   C. mob rule
    B. submission   D. low class   (C)

oddling (od′ling)
    A. cozen   C. odd
    B. crow   D. basking   (C)

offal (ô′fəl, of′əl)
    A. garbage   C. external
    B. wicked   D. eccentric   (A)

omniana (om·nē·an′ə)
    A. fete   C. kleptomania
    B. utopia   D. notations   (D)

omophagic (ō''mə·faj′ik)
    A. visionary   C. eager
    B. ancestral   D. eating raw flesh   (D)

145

omphalos (om'fə·ləs)
    A. black eye   C. navel
    B. buttock   D. big toe   (C)

omphaloskepsis (om"fə·lō·skep'sis-)
    A. expulsion   C. overthrow
    B. stimulation   D. contemplation   (D)

onanism (ō'nə·niz"əm)
    A. solitary   C. materialism
    B. masturbation   C. masochism   (B)

oneiric (ō·nī'rik)
    A. of dreams   C. very loud
    B. hulky   D. conspicuous   (A)

operose (op'ə·rōs")
    A. heavy   C. viscid
    B. laborious   D. wasteful   (B)

opposable (ə·pō'zə·bəl)
    A. resistible   C. proud
    B. sinful   D. contrary   (A)

oppugnant (ə·pug'nənt)
    A. fowl   C. unclean
    B. opposing   D. uncouth   (B)

orgulous (ôr'gyə·ləs)
    A. haughty   C. jubilant
    B. longish   D. moist   (A)

origami (ôr"ə·gä'mē)
    A. awkward   C. Japanese art form
    B. game   D. mouth disease   (C)

orotund (ōr'ə·tund", ôr'-)
    A. resonant   C. massive
    B. horned   D. oblong   (A)

osseocarnisanguineoviscericartilaginonervomedullary (good luck)
    A. bone disease   C. idol worship
    B. common cold   D. human body   (D)

ostreoid (ôs'trē·oid")
    A. southerly   C. oyster-like
    B. corvine   D. bespectacled   (C)

ostrobogulous (os·trə·bog'yə·ləs)
    A. wicked   C. furry
    B. pithy   D. an oath   (D)

oubliette (o͞o·blē·et')
    A. courtesy   C. napkin
    B. jewel   D. dungeon   (D)

overweening (ō"vər·wē'ning)
    A. arrogant   C. dependent
    B. tyro   D. motherly   (A)

paedophage (pā'dō·fāj, pē"-)
    A. worker   C. flagship
    B. child-eater   D. waiter   (B)

palindrome (pal'in·drōm")
    A. amphitheatre   C. jeep
    B. bungler   D. word oddity   (D)

pall (pôl)
    A. become dull   C. to tug
    B. white   D. not fearful   (A)

pandurate (pan'dyə·rāt")
    A. fiddle-shaped   C. look for gold
    B. gaudy   D. resolute   (A)

pannier (pan'yər, -ē·ər)
    A. bread box   C. basket
    B. frock   D. shovel   (C)

panjandrum (pan·jan'drəm)
    A. ministry   C. Chinese dish
    B. pompous official   D. a stew   (B)

paphian (pā'fē·ən)
    A. liberal   C. erotic
    B. whimsical   D. hairless   (C)

paraclete (par'ə·klēt")
    A. soldier   C. sham
    B. an advocate   D. Indian bird   (B)

paraenetic (par·ə·net'ik)
    A. advisory   C. vexed
    B. dismal   D. crippled   (A)

147

pasquinade (pas″kwə·nād′)
    A. a walk
    B. lampoon
    C. praise
    D. party   (B)

pavid (pav′id)
    A. afraid
    B. ornate
    C. sincere
    D. honest   (A)

pelagic (pə·laj′ik)
    A. resolute
    B. oceanic
    C. modest
    D. weak   (B)

penetralia (pen″i·trā′lē·ə)
    A. inner recess
    B. cavern
    C. long trail
    D. intense affair   (A)

periclitate (pə′ri·klə·tāt″)
    A. endanger
    B. unreal
    C. falsetto
    D. concur   (A)

periphrastic (per″ə·fras′tik)
    A. pleased
    B. engulf
    C. fed on
    D. verbose   (D)

perspicuous (per·spik′yōō·əs)
    A. feeble
    B. lucid
    C. muddy
    D. sticky   (B)

pharisaical (far″i·sā′i·kəl)
    A. useless
    B. pitiful
    C. cowardly
    D. sanctimonious   (D)

philotheoparoptesism (good luck)
    A. human sacrifice
    B. Christ-killing
    C. religious doctrine
    D. idol worship   (A)

philluminist (fi·lōōm′ə·nist)
    A. violinist
    B. matchbox top collector
    C. minor official
    D. theologian   (B)

philter (fil′tər)
    A. veil
    B. trifle
    C. pale
    D. love potion   (D)

phobophobia (fō′bō·fō′bē·ə)
    A. alarmed
    B. neutral
    C. fear of fear
    D. fear of light   (C)

148

phocomelia (fō″kō·mē′lē·ə)
    A. frail   C. notched
    B. birth defect   D. fire-eater   **(B)**

piacular (pī·ak′yə·lər)
    A. feudal   C. thoughtful
    B. restless   D. expiatory   **(D)**

piliferous (pī·lif′ər·əs)
    A. feeble   C. ill
    B. vocal   D. having hair   **(D)**

pinchbeck (pinch′bek″)
    A. supporter   C. sham
    B. effete   D. former   **(C)**

pinguescent (ping·gwes′ənt)
    A. growing fat   C. ball-shaped
    B. ferocious   D. ominous   **(A)**

pinguid (ping′gwid)
    A. fervid   C. stable
    B. greasy   D. pink   **(B)**

platypod (plat′i·pod)
    A. fallen arches   C. linguist
    B. an animal   D. micro-organism   **(A)**

pleonastic (plē″ə·nas′tik)
    A. morbid   C. redundancy
    B. plastic   D. public   **(C)**

pneumonoultramicroscopicsilicovolcanoconiosis (good luck)
    A. micro-organism   C. penicillin
    B. lung disease   D. space flight   **(B)**

polychrestic (pol″ē·krest′ik)
    A. meager   C. bright and shining
    B. having many uses ′   D. midget-like   **(B)**

polyhistor (pol″ē·his′tər)
    A. sect   C. tube
    B. scholar   D. cathode   **(B)**

popinjay (pop′in·jā″)
    A. bird   C. flower
    B. coxcomb   D. tool   **(B)**

149

popliteal (pop·lit′ē·əl, pop″li·tē′əl)
    A. of fish nets   C. rife
    B. back of the knee   D. thorny   **(B)**

posset (pos′it)
    A. harness   C. a blend
    B. a drink   D. recover   **(B)**

postprandial (pōst·pran′dē·əl)
    A. after meals   C. spittle
    B. tardy   D. after a boat race   **(A)**

pot-valiant (pot′val″yənt)
    A. moderate   C. brave from drink
    B. spurious   D. use of drugs   **(C)**

primoprime (prīm′ō·prīm)
    A. first coat   C. foremost
    B. pump   D. proper   **(C)**

procrustean (prō·krus′tē·ən)
    A. causing uniformity   C. before lunch
    B. preparing for meals D. violent   **(A)**

profluent (prof′lōō·ənt)
    A. flowing smoothly   C. making profit
    B. scanty   D. for public use   **(A)**

propaedeutic (prō″pi·dōō′tik, -dyōō′-)
    A. urgent   C. introductory
    B. risky   D. sparse   **(C)**

psittacistic (sit″ə·siz′tik)
    A. of moles   C. specious
    B. of lice   D. mechanical speech **(D)**

puerperal (pyōō·ur′pər·əl)
    A. of groups   C. mutinous
    B. religious   D. in labor   **(D)**

pukka (puk′ə)
    A. first-rate   C. submission
    B. blush   D. of hockey   **(A)**

pullulate (pul′yə·lāt″)
    A. neglect   C. rank
    B. ridicule   D. breed   **(D)**

pulvinate (pul'və·nāt")
   A. hasten
   B. smuggle

   C. cushion-shaped
   D. abduct   (C)

pursive (pur'siv, pər'-)
   A. out of breath
   B. worldly

   C. introspective
   D. small and tight   (A)

purulent (pyoor'ə·lənt, pyoor'yə-)
   A. incline
   B. of pus

   C. unwilling
   D. of purity   (B)

putsch (pooch)
   A. cassock
   B. uprising

   C. picture
   D. furniture   (B)

quadrumanous (kwo·droo'mə·nəs)
   A. four-handed
   B. ethical

   C. four rooms
   D. four days   (A)

quail (kwāl)
   A. unpack
   B. steep

   C. a bird
   D. cower   (D)

quercine (kwur'sin, -sīn)
   A. of oaks
   B. flaccid

   C. drooping
   D. fatty   (A)

querist (kwēr'ist)
   A. teacher
   B. questioner

   C. thinker
   D. naturalist   (B)

quiddity (kwid'i·tē)
   A. vigor
   B. lingo

   C. nationality
   D. the essence   (D)

ramiform (ram'ə·fôrm")
   A. glossy
   B. reddish

   C. branch-like
   D. laureate   (C)

ranine (rā'nīn, rə·nīn')
   A. frog-like
   B. sexy

   C. blunt
   D. semicircular   (A)

raptorial (rap·tōr'ē·əl, -tôr'-)
   A. abusive
   B. predatory

   C. instructive
   D. cloying   (B)

151

rasorial (rə·sōr′ē·əl, -sôr′-)
    A. scratching for food   C. sharp
    B. clever   D. of nests   (A)

refluent (ref′lo͞o·ənt)
    A. mixed   C. ebbing
    B. stuttering   D. loose   (C)

refocillate (re·fos′ə·lāt″)
    A. stock   C. revive
    B. deny   D. disavow   (C)

remontant (ri·mon′tənt)
    A. stubborn   C. flowering again
    B. climbing   D. climbing higher   (C)

renitent (ri·nīt′ənt, ren′i·tənt)
    A. recalcitrant   C. of dye
    B. publish   D. clean   (A)

retund (ri·tund′)
    A. adhere   C. stem
    B. weaken   D. graft   (B)

rhadamanthine (rad″ə·man′thin)
    A. inert   C. vital
    B. honest   D. erroneous   (B)

rhapsodist (rap′sə·dist)
    A. musician   C. beau
    B. cripple   D. enthusiast   (D)

rhombic (rom′bik)
    A. circular   C. diamond-shaped
    B. stringy   D. ovoid   (C)

rhyparography (rī″pə·rog′rə·fē)
    A. slander   C. handwriting
    B. study of weather D painting sordid pictures (D)

rimose (rī′mōs, rī·mōs′)
    A. colorful   C. chinked
    B. dual   D. musical   (C)

rodomontade (rod″ə·mon·tād′, rō″də-)
    A. bragging   C. beauty
    B. piety   D. peace   (A)

roil (roil)
    A. coil   C. bisect
    B. roll   D. irritate   (D)

roisterer (roi′stər·ər)
    A. clown   C. idolater
    B. noisy reveler   D. politician   (B)

rugose (rōō′gōs, rōō·gōs′)
    A. wrinkled   C. old
    B. bland   D. reddish   (A)

sabulous (sab′yə·ləs)
    A. truthful   C. safe
    B. sandy   D. sordid   (B)

sacculate (sak′yə·lāt″)
    A. mistaken   C. filtered
    B. sac-like   D. divulge   (B)

sanguisugent (sang·gwi′sə·gənt)
    A. insecure   C. confident
    B. soothing   D. bloodsucking   (D)

sapid (sap′id, -īd)
    A. savory   C. foolish
    B. haughty   D. nervous   (A)

sarcoid (sar′koid)
    A. blunt   C. fleshy
    B. ripe   D. spiral   (C)

sardanapalian (sär″də·nə·pāl′yən)
    A. oriental   C. husky
    B. effeminate   D. vast   (B)

saturnalia (sat″ər·nā′lē·ə, -nal′yə)
    A. discord   C. of clouds
    B. planetary   D. an orgy   (D)

satyriasis (sat″ə·rī′ə·sis)
    A. of holidays   C. terror
    B. rampant sexual desire   D. vampire   (B)

saurian (sôr′ē·ən)
    A. sour   C. floating
    B. tender   D. lizard-like   (D)

153

scabrous (skab'rəs)
    A. abusive   C. extrinsic
    B. rough   D. dirty   (B)

scacchic (ska'kik)
    A. of chess   C. thorny
    B. pimpled   D. tender   (A)

scaphoid (skaf'oid)
    A. boat-shaped   C. curled
    B. of iron   D. shell   (A)

sciolism (sī'ə·liz"əm)
    A. swelling   C. of gems
    B. pretense of knowledge   D. study of the mind   (B)

scout (skout)
    A. plead   C. survey
    B. seed   D. flout   (D)

scribacious (skri·bā'shəs)
    A. servile   C. inclined to acne
    B. fond of writing   D. talkative   (B)

scrofulous (skrof'yə·ləs)
    A. artful   C. bald
    B. beauteous   D. degenerate   (D)

scud (skud)
    A. sink   C. lordly
    B. dart nimbly   D. scrub with vigor   (B)

scungilaginous (skun·ji·la'jə·nəs)
    A. of worts   C. of dirty ears
    B. gelatinous   D. heavy with child   (B)

sectile (sek'til)
    A. corrupt   C. divisive
    B. cutable   D. abrasive   (B)

sedentarize (sed·ən'tə·rīz)
    A. pliant   C. electrocute
    B. slovenly   D. settle   (D)

semiotic (sē"mē·ot'ik, -mī-)
    A. brainy   C. stealthy
    B. causing pains   D. of signs   (D)

154

sempiternal (sem″pi·tur′nəl)
    A. occasionally
    B. caustic

    C. of pits
    D. everlasting   (D)

senescent (sə·nes′ənt)
    A. delaying
    B. aging

    C. discovering
    D. sleeping   (B)

septentrional (sep·ten′trē·ə·nəl)
    A. of fall
    B. five-fold

    C. wintry
    D. northern   (D)

sequacious (si·kwā′shəs)
    A. surrender
    B. servile

    C. defect
    D. humiliate   (B)

seraphic (si·raf′ik)
    A. angelic
    B. inert

    C. forsaken
    D. artless   (A)

sericeous (si·rish′əs)
    A. infected
    B. scarred

    C. silvery
    D. silky   (D)

serried (ser′ēd)
    A. hidden
    B. closely packed

    C. with fringe
    D. displayed   (B)

shard (shärd)
    A. ruler
    B. soldier

    C. basket weave
    D. broken earthenware   (D)

shmooish (shmoo′ish)
    A. grubby
    B. Semitic

    C. rectangular
    D. balloon-like   (D)

sibylline (sib′ə·lēn″, -līn″)
    A. wise
    B. prophetic

    C. nubile
    D. fat and sassy   (B)

siffilate (sif′ə·lāt″)
    A. to sift
    B. coughing

    C. diseased
    D. to whisper   (D)

simony (sī′mə·nē, sim′ə-)
    A. district
    B. wordplay

    C. merchanting sacred things
    D. food list   (C)

simper (sim′pər)
    A. cry
    B. smirk

    C. steam
    D. sift
    (B)

sinerous (si′nə·rəs)
    A. vile
    B. honest

    C. snake-like
    D. craven
    (C)

sisyphean (sis″ə·fē′ən)
    A. heroic
    B. unavailing

    C. confident
    D. cursed
    (B)

sjambok (sham·bok′, -buk′)
    A. a whip
    B. insect

    C. small deer
    D. plant fiber
    (A)

skein (skān)
    A. battle
    B. coiled yarn

    C. line of poetry
    D. a plan
    (B)

slough (slou)
    A. trap door
    B. swamp

    C. impasse
    D. sled
    (B)

snollygoster (snol′ē·gos″tər)
    A. lie
    B. impostor

    C. shrewd person
    D. organ
    (C)

sodality (sō·dal′i·tē, sə-)
    A. fellowship
    B. clique

    C. union
    D. of cartels
    (A)

solon (sō′lən)
    A. den
    B. wise men

    C. solitary
    D. hay bin
    (B)

soodle (sood′əl)
    A. flinch
    B. drawl

    C. coddle
    D. saunter
    (D)

sough (sou, suf)
    A. hail
    B. beat

    C. murmur
    D. wound
    (C)

spatulate (spach′ə·lit, -lāt″)
    A. expedite
    B. argue

    C. hasten
    D. broadened
    (D)

spawling (spô'ling)
    A. causing friction   C. throat-clearing
    B. work with wood   D. crying   (C)

spumescent (spyōō·mes'ənt)
    A. white   C. livid
    B. overflowing   D. foamy   (D)

squamous (skwā'məs)
    A. afraid   C. speckled
    B. scaly   D. of squares   (B)

stagorium (sta·gôr'ē·um)
    A. zoo   C. opus
    B. rendezvous   D. Camelot   (B)

stakhanovite (stə·kä'nə·vīt″, -kan'ə-)
    A. hobo   C. diligent worker
    B. soldier   D. one who stacks wood   (C)

steatopygous (stē″ə·tō·pī'gəs, -top'ə-)
    A. spoon-billed   C. buxom
    B. fat-rumped   D. ripe   (B)

stele (stē'lē, stēl)
    A. officer   C. mineral
    B. pillar   D. gravestone   (D)

sternutation (stur″nyə·tā'shən)
    A. defiance   C. a withdrawing
    B. sneeze   D. cough   (B)

stertorous (stur'tər·əs)
    A. snoring   C. strong
    B. of stealth   D. ponderous   (A)

strepitous (strep'i·təs)
    A. striped   C. hollow
    B. noisy   D. lanky   (B)

stridulate (strij'ə·lāt″)
    A. quiver   C. vault
    B. striped   D. chirp   (D)

struthionine (strōō'thē·ə·nīn″)
    A. of beer   C. of apes
    B. ribbon-like   D. ostrich-like   (D)

stultiloquence (stul·təl'ə·kwəns)
    A. babble   C. bickering
    B. displeasure   D. approval   (A)

succose (sə'kōs)
    A. sweet   C. loud
    B. juicy   D. loving   (B)

succubus (suk'yə·bəs)
    A. impediment   C. demon
    B. statue   D. juicy   (C)

succussion (sə·kush'ən)
    A. reflection   C. impact
    B. shaking   D. noise   (B)

suctorial (suk·tōr'ē·əl, -tôr'-)
    A. of sucking   C. repressive
    B. ductile   D. loose   (A)

suffuse (sə·fyo͞oz')
    A. pardon   C. turn off
    B. spread over   D. infer   (B)

supernal (soo·pur'nəl)
    A. expert   C. savage
    B. extra   D. divine   (D)

supine (so͞o·pīn')
    A. suave   C. soft
    B. sluggish   D. flat   (B)

suppositive (sə·poz'i·tiv)
    A. false   C. supporting
    B. internal   D. conjectural   (D)

sutteeism (su·tē'ism, sut'ē·ism)
    A. immolation   C. divination
    B. seance   D. Oriental sect   (A)

swale (swāl)
    A. aloud   C. blow
    B. sigh   D. moist hollow   (D)

synergistic (sin″ər·jis'tik)
    A. senile   C. strategic
    B. splenetic   D. cooperating   (D)

tabescent (tə·bes′ənt)
    A. tedious
    B. taciturn
    C. static
    D. withering   **(D)**

tachygraphy (ta·kig′rə·fē, tə-)
    A. type
    B. shorthand
    C. printer's measure
    D. of maps   **(B)**

tarboosh (tär·boosh′)
    A. fez
    B. tulip
    C. spouse
    D. plant   **(A)**

tectonic (tek·ton′ik)
    A. supple
    B. solemn
    C. of cowardice
    D. of construction   **(D)**

temblor (tem′blər, -blôr)
    A. mixing glass
    B. suburb
    C. earthquake
    D. cupboard   **(C)**

temerarious (tem″ə·rār′ē·əs)
    A. wary
    B. rash
    C. timid
    D. wondering   **(B)**

tessellated (tes′ə·lā″tid)
    A. cloven
    B. bald
    C. checkered
    D. spirited   **(C)**

thalassic (thə·las′ik)
    A. subtle
    B. of inland seas
    C. adorned with splendor
    D. passive   **(B)**

thanatopsis (than″ə·top′sis)
    A. fertilizer mulch
    B. toupee
    C. phylum
    D. musing on death   **(D)**

thaumaturgic (thô″mə·tur′jik)
    A. chemical
    B. magical
    C. indiscreet
    D. of water power   **(B)**

thersitical (thər·sit′i·kəl)
    A. foul-mouthed
    B. jaunty
    C. whimsical
    D. grandiose   **(A)**

thetical (thet′ə·kəl)
    A. heretical
    B. orthodox
    C. cloudy
    D. set forth   **(D)**

159

theurgic (thē·ur'jik)
    A. magical   C. powerful
    B. restrained   D. relevant   (A)

thewless (thyo͞o'lis)
    A. strong   C. without thistles
    B. without vigor   D. seedless   (B)

thrasonical (thrā·son'i·kəl)
    A. boastful   C. tipsy
    B. bashful   D. evasive   (A)

titivate (tit'ə·vāt'')
    A. spruce up   C. stimulate
    B. oppose   D. infuse   (A)

titubant (tich'oo·bənt)
    A. perky   C. passive
    B. staggering   D. nasty   (B)

tohu-bohu (tō'ho͞o·bō'ho͞o)
    A. hell   C. chaos
    B. paradise   D. discipline   (C)

totipalmate (tō''tə·pal'mit, -māt)
    A. stunted   C. fraternal
    B. webbed   D. finished   (B)

tramontane (trə·mon'tān)
    A. easterly   C. foreign
    B. bilking   D. flowery   (C)

transcalent (trans·kā'lənt)
    A. tubular   C. transmitting heat
    B. underground   D. across the desert   (C)

transude (tran·so͞od')
    A. surround   C. confide
    B. pass through   D. unbosom   (B)

trice (trīs)
    A. three-fold   C. game
    B. larva   D. an instant   (D)

triskaidekaphobia (tri''skə·dekə·fō'bē·ə)
    A. shocked   C. aversion to Dekes
    B. fear of 13   D. fear of worms   (B)

triturate (trich′ə·rāt″)
A. mellow   C. grow moldy
B. grind   D. decay   (B)
troglodyte (trog′lə·dīt″)
A. harness   C. wheel
B. fossil   D. caveman   (D)
truckle (truk′əl)
A. disdain   C. sparkle
B. servile   D. convey   (B)
turbinate (tur′bə·nit, -nāt″)
A. whorled   C. clothed
B. final   D. electrical   (A)
turgescent (tur·jes′ənt)
A. rigorous   C. swelling
B. opening   D. melting   (C)
ubiety (yōō·bī′i·tē)
A. girth   C. presence
B. located   D. platitude   (B)
ufologist (yōō·fol′ə·jist)
A. biologist   C. tree expert
B. clumsy person   D. skyward gazer   (D)
ukase (yōō′kās, yōō·kāz′)
A. decree   C. surrealistic
B. despair   D. portfolio   (A)
ulotrichous (yōō·lo′trə·kəs)
A. having curly hair   C. short and dumpy
B. blithe   D. of ringworms   (A)
ultracrepidarian (ul·trə·kre·pə·dâr′ē·ən)
A. extreme   C. owl
B. overstepping   D. senile   (B)
ululate (yōōl′yə·lāt″, ul′-)
A. encroach   C. mislead
B. howl   D. beckon   (B)
umbrageous (um·brā′jəs)
A. shady   C. lucrative
B. ugly   D. fallacious   (A)

161

unbosom (un·booz'əm, -bōō'zəm)

A. excise	C. strip
B. disclose	D. cut	(B)

unciform (un·sə·fôrm')

A. smooth	C. round
B. hook-shaped	D. of tails	(B)

unguiculate (ung·gwik'yə·lit, -lāt'')

A. claw-like	C. scudding
B. horned	D. of cows	(A)

untoward (un·tōrd', -tôrd')

A. unfortunate	C. distinguished
B. blithe	D. creative	(A)

unwonted (un·wōn'tid, -wôn'-)

A. unusual	C. austere
B. disliked	D. hated	(A)

uranic (yoo·ran'ik)

A. of kidneys	C. celestial
B. furious	D. flaccid	(C)

urceolate (ur'sē·ə·lit, -lāt'')

A. flap	C. remiss
B. bear-like	D. pitcher-shaped	(D)

ustulate (us'chə·lit, -lāt'')

A. naked	C. milky
B. wet	D. scorched	(D)

utriculate (yōō·trik'yə·lit, -lāt'')

A. of podiums	C. bland
B. bag-like	D. wizened	(B)

vaticinal (və·tis'ə·nəl)

A. religious	C. spacious
B. of cups	D. prophetic	(D)

velleity (və·lē'i·tē)

A. a mere wish	C. dispensation
B. mythological god	D. lotus position	(A)

vellicate (vel'ə·kāt'')

A. define	C. twinkle
B. pluck	D. allot	(B)

162

velutinous (və·lōōt'ə·nəs)
    A. velvety   C. rich
    B. cloudy   D. sour   (A)

venatic (vē·nat'ik)
    A. of blood   C. lustful
    B. tributary   D. of hunting   (D)

ventricous (ven'trə·kos'')
    A. unwilling   C. hostile
    B. protuberant   D. dorsal   (B)

verecund (ver'ə·kund'')
    A. truthful   C. identical
    B. bashful   D. blind   (B)

vespertine (ves'pər·tin, -tīn'')
    A. divided   C. windy
    B. peaceful   D. of evening   (D)

vespine (ves'pīn, -pin)
    A. wasp-like   C. elite
    B. industrial   D. ambitious   (A)

vestiary (ves'tē·er''ē)
    A. inherent   C. geological
    B. of dress   D. of veils   (B)

vesticate (ves'tə·kāt'')
    A. harden   C. corrode
    B. reveal   D. blister   (D)

viatic (vī·at'ik)
    A. frenzied   C. of a road
    B. ritualistic   D. vile   (C)

vicenary (vis'ə·ner''ē)
    A. colonial   C. rootless
    B. official   D. twenty   (D)

vicinal (vis'ə·nəl)
    A. adjacent   C. transitional
    B. oily   D. kingly   (A)

villatic (vi·lat'ik)
    A. compact   C. alarmed
    B. rural   D. urban   (B)

vimineous (vi·min′ē·əs)
  A. jealous   C. woven of twigs
  B. notable   D. elementary   **(C)**

virgate (vur′git, -gāt)
  A. rod-like   C. coarse
  B. pure and chaste   D. indented   **(A)**

vivisepulture (viv″ə·sep′əl·chər)
  A. talkative woman   C. lively speech
  B. stillborn   D. bury alive   **(D)**

volant (vō′lənt)
  A. flying   C. voluntary
  B. constrained   D. volatile   **(A)**

warren (wôr′ən, wor′-)
  A. excuse   C. restraint
  B. permit   D. tenement   **(D)**

wazoo (wä′zōō)
  A. vivarium   C. scream
  B. fundament   D. bird whistle   **(B)**

winnow (win′ō)
  A. tie up   C. evict
  B. sift   D. hesitate   **(B)**

wonted (wōn′tid, wôn′-)
  A. forgotten   C. temporary
  B. base   D. customary   **(D)**

wraith (rāth)
  A. bond   C. alien
  B. ghost   D. tree ornament   **(B)**

xerophagy (zi·rof′ə·jē)
  A. earning nothing   C. hungry
  B. broke   D. eating dry food   **(D)**

xiphoid (zif′oid)
  A. sword-shaped   C. sour like a lemon
  B. square   D. pungent   **(A)**

zonule (zōn′yōōl)
  A. bud   C. atmospheric
  B. foreign   D. small band   **(D)**

autonomasia, 37
avatar, 37
azure, 80

balneal, 61
banausic, 62
bandersnatch, 90
bastinado, 52
batten, 52
bay, 79
beetling, 62
beldam, 37
belletristic, 84
berylline, 81
bezoardic, 62
bibelot, 37
bight, 37
billingsgate, 84
bisque, 80
blandishment, 37
bombinate, 52
borborology, 90
bosky, 62
brazen, 20
brindled, 82
bromidrosis, 28
brouhaha, 37
brumal, 62
brummagem, 62
buccal, 28
buff, 80
buncombe, 84
burlesque, 52
bursiform, 20
bushido, 38
bustluscious, 96

cachinnation, 90
cadaverous, 81

cadge, 53
caducous, 62
cairn, 38
caitiff, 62
calescent, 62
caliginous, 62
calligraphy, 38
callipygous, 28
calumet, 38
camarilla, 38
campanulate, 20
canary, 81
candent, 62
canny, 62
caparison, 53
caprylic, 62
captious, 62
carbecue, 96
carbuncle, 79
carious, 62
carking, 62
carillon, 38
carmine, 80
carousal, 38
caryatid, 38
caterwaul, 53
cathexis, 38
caudate, 20
caudle, 38
causerie, 38
celestine, 80
ceraceous, 21
cerebration, 28
cerise, 80
cernuous, 21
charnel, 39
chiastic, 63
chiromancy, 39
chthonic, 63
cimmerian, 84
cinerary, 63
circadian, 63
cleave, 63

169

173

174

175